What Makes Us Whole

What Makes Us Whole

Finding God in Contemporary Life

Noel Cooper

LITURGICAL PRESS

Collegeville, Minnesota

www.litpress.org

Cover design by Ann Blattner.

1   2   3   4   5   6   7   8   9

Library of Congress Cataloging-in-Publication Data

Cooper, Noel.
    What makes us whole : finding God in contemporary life /
Noel Cooper.
        p. cm.
      ISBN 978-0-8146-3289-5 (pbk.)
    1. Spirituality.   I. Title.

BV4501.3.C6675   2009
248—dc22   2009018342

For Andrew, Paul, and John

Your quest for wholeness
encourages all who love you.

The Spirit helps us in our weakness;

for we do not know how to pray as we ought,

but that very Spirit intercedes

with sighs too deep for words.

And God, who searches the heart,

knows what is the mind of the Spirit.

(Romans 8:26-27)

Contents

Introduction

Life is a journey in search of wholeness.

From our earliest moments until our last conscious breath we are building the person we are. Sometimes consciously and sometimes with very little awareness, day after day, year after year, we are shaping our *selves* by the choices we make.[1] Always we are influenced by other people, by events, by forces in our world. But ultimately we must take responsibility for who we are as we seek to be true to ourselves, to find peace of heart: to become whole.

"Wholeness" is a profound word expressing the goal of the human journey. After Jesus healed a suffering person he would sometimes say: "Your faith has made you whole."[2] The religious word "holiness" derives from the same root as "wholeness" and has the same meaning. To the extent that we are true to ourselves, we are faithful to God: holy. Wholeness means completeness, fullness of life, holiness.

---

[1] This way of speaking about moral responsibility was borrowed more than thirty years ago from John Giles Milhaven's book, *Towards a New Catholic Morality* (New York: Doubleday, 1972).

[2] The Greek word *sesoken* (See Mark 5:34; Luke 7:50; 8:48; 17:19) can be translated "made you whole," "made you well," "healed you," or "saved you." Try to have all those meanings in mind when you read the word "wholeness." The introduction to the "Wholeness" section of this book will elaborate on the meaning of the term.

The human journey, then, is a quest. The term "quest" evokes timeless symbols of journeying and searching. The trials of life and our personal shortcomings ensure that wholeness will always remain an objective rather than an accomplishment. We are wounded voyagers, always seeking to overcome obstacles and to persevere in pursuit of our true self. As we travel we reflect on our progress, reaffirm our purpose, and reshape the path we are following.

What do we need to reach our true destiny, to achieve wholeness? This book will blend the insights of the Bible with the concerns and insights of contemporary believers, and will discuss our life's journey in search of wholeness and the role of God in that journey.

In the first section of the book we will consider five of the elements that contribute to wholeness or fullness of life for human beings: loving and being loved, a sense of purpose, a consistent personal value system, freedom, and emotional well-being.

The Good News is that we do not have to achieve wholeness by our own efforts. *God*'s part in our quest for wholeness is described by the word "salvation." Jesus' saying, "your faith has made you whole," can also be translated as "your faith has saved you." Salvation and wholeness are different words for the same reality. The term "salvation" refers not primarily to life after death, but to the action of God now: God saves us while we live. In the journey of our lives, God intervenes as a spiritual power and leads us toward wholeness. God enables us to respond to the situations we face in life as free and responsible people. God helps us to make sense of our lives, to be wise, to live in love, to make good choices, and to have the courage to do what is right. We believe that if we open our hearts to God's action (or "saving power") and build our lives with God's help we can grow toward fullness of life—*no matter what happens* in the course of our lives. "God saves us" means "God reaches into our lives and leads us to wholeness."

The second section of the book will attempt to describe how God affects our quest for wholeness. Part of that discussion will express dissatisfaction with some traditional ways of speaking about God that seem unsatisfactory or incredible to many adults. Only by facing the difficult questions can we maintain a spirit of faith in the face of life's difficulties and contemporary challenges to faith.

This book is addressed to a wide range of intelligent contemporary believers, and especially to parents who hope to express the value of faith to their children. Many readers may have had some early education about believing but now find that the traditional expressions of faith they learned as children do not respond to their adult need to reflect on the meaning of the human journey. Others may have continued to learn about the Gospel proclamation as adults and wish to explore various points of view about familiar and difficult questions. The book is written from a Christian perspective but is not intended to present the teaching of any one denomination. It is meant to be understandable even to those who may be quite unfamiliar with the language of theology.

What Makes Us Whole is the product of more than thirty years' experience as a husband and member of a "parenting team" and an equally long career as a teacher of students and adults in the field of Religious Education in Roman Catholic schools in Canada. Significant additional experience was gained after retirement, when I participated in a (non-religious) parenting program for fathers of young children. Working with groups of men whose only requirement for participation was being the father of a child under the age of six, I met hundreds of dads who discussed their hopes and dreams for their children and the problems they faced in trying to be good parents.

An early form of this book was written in the months following the death of my beloved wife Patricia in 2002. At that time I began to write about my efforts to find the hand of God in the illness and untimely death of this vibrant woman, a noble mother and teacher. With the devoted help of our three sons and their beloved life partners our family survived a period of mourning that continues still, but we have all managed to go forward with our lives in a manner that can be described as a continuing journey toward wholeness in a spirit of peacefulness. This book is dedicated to our three wonderful sons, Andrew, Paul, and John. Together we are family in the best sense possible.

Of course, few people can thrive in loneliness. Before and after the death of their mother, Andrew, Paul, and John found and committed themselves to loving and supportive women, Lauren, Sarah, and Kate. The most surprising outcome, however, was reserved for me. About a year after Patricia's death, by the most unexpected coincidence, I renewed acquaintance with a woman, also named Pat, whom I had known through the decade of the 1960s. She too had been married and widowed. We had not seen each other for more than thirty years when Pat happened to encounter mutual friends (whom she had not seen for many years either) as they strolled past a booth she was staffing at an autumn fair. Our friends told me about their chance encounter; Pat and I made contact; and fifteen months later we married at the age of 66. We are enjoying happy and peaceful lives in retirement and feel immensely grateful for the good fortune that brought us together.

To return to the theme of the second section of this book, I believe that my remarriage is an important part of our whole family's journey toward wholeness (in a deeply religious sense). I give thanks for this great blessing, but I do not believe literally that God brought Pat and me together any more than I believe God caused or could have prevented the death of my late wife, Patricia, before she reached the age of 60. We have to find a way of understanding the role of God in our lives, in good times and in bad. That search for faith and wholeness is the subject of this book.

PART ONE

What Makes Us Whole

Your faith has made you well.
(Mark 5:34)

Life is a journey in search of wholeness. But what does "wholeness" mean? A number of synonyms may help us understand the meaning of the word more fully.

Modern popular psychology uses a word that derives from the same root word when it speaks of "wellness" or well-being. When Jesus healed people, often he concluded with a phrase that is now usually translated as "your faith has made you well." Other translations use the word "whole" in that quotation, because "to be whole" means to be well, to be in touch with one's true self, to be growing toward fulfillment.

"Peace of heart" is another phrase with a similar meaning. The Jewish greeting *shalom* ("peace"), though often used as unreflectively as our "goodbye" (meaning "God be with you"), speaks of deep inner peacefulness. Jesus refers to the deeper meaning of *shalom* in John's narrative of the Last Supper when he says: "my peace I give to you. I do not give to you as the world gives" (John 14:27). The peace Jesus gives is what we mean by wholeness.

It is possible to be a peaceful person in the face of tragedy and oppressive circumstances. On the other hand, some situations can destroy or seriously weaken a person's peace of heart. When a person becomes less peaceful, to that extent the person's journey toward wholeness has been hindered. Our quest for wholeness is essentially a quest for inner peace.

We mentioned in the introduction that wholeness and holiness are synonyms. To the extent that we are true to ourselves we are faithful to God, and therefore "holy." The Gospel according to John uses the term "fullness of life" to express the meaning of "wholeness" in terms that are distinctive to that gospel: "I came that they may have life, and have it abundantly" (John 10:10).

The last word in this series of near-synonyms is "happiness." What does it take to make human beings happy?

Early in the twenty-first century, discussions about happiness are plentiful. Some, like this one, are conducted in religious terms. Others are based in psychology. The work of Dr. Martin Seligman[1] is based on his insight that while psychology has understandably devoted itself to the problems people face, it should also emphasize the sources of happiness in people's lives. Seligman's work identifies a number of factors that contribute to human happiness and encourages readers to recognize and appreciate them in their own lives.

Wholeness, wellness, well-being, peace of heart, holiness, happiness: these are all terms that describe in slightly different ways the goal of life's quest.

To the extent that we are believers, our quest for wholeness is built on the foundation of faith. Faith is supposed to support and strengthen us as we search for personal fulfillment, for well-being, for peace of heart, for happiness. Faith helps us understand what wholeness involves, and faith assures us that we do

---

[1] Martin E. Seligman, *Authentic Happiness* (New York: Simon and Schuster, 2002).

Dr. Seligman's website is also interesting: http://www.authentichappiness.sas.upenn.edu.

not have to achieve wholeness only by our own efforts: God's saving energy strengthens us and leads us forward on our quest. We will discuss God's role in our journey in the second half of this book.

In this first section we will consider some of the elements that contribute to wholeness, holiness, wellness, well-being, peace of heart, and happiness in an individual human life. No doubt there are dozens of possible factors. In the following chapters you are invited to consider only these five elements of wholeness:

- Knowing that you are loved is the indispensable cornerstone of personal growth.

- Everyone should be aware of, and periodically reconsider and reaffirm, a sense of purpose in life: a focus for all one's activities, a sense of direction.

- We are forming ourselves by the decisions we make. Living consistently according to a personal value system is an important element of growing toward wholeness.

- All of us desire to be free, to set the course of our own lives. God supports human freedom.

- Emotional well-being is essential to human wholeness.

Chapter One

Knowing You Are Loved

Love is the most precious possible gift one person can give to another. It is an essential element of human wholeness. Knowing that you are loved, being able to express love for someone else, and accepting love from others are part of the foundation of every successful human life.

Love is a transforming gift. If someone says "I love you" for the first time, you are a new person. You become capable of things you never knew you could do. When someone says "I love you" over and over again, in word and action, the feeling within you is a perfect ambience for pursuing your quest for wholeness. Further, love is creative. Besides the obvious truth that love can lead to the creation of new lives, love brings forth all kinds of creative juices in lover and beloved. In the face of loss or profound injury, love heals in the form of comfort or forgiveness.

Our religious tradition strongly affirms the value of love. "You shall love your neighbor as yourself" (Lev 19:18) was identified by Jesus (and many rabbis) as the second-most-important commandment in the entire Law of Moses, which included 613 laws. Jesus' own teaching is reported in the Gospel of John: "Just as I have loved you, you also should love one another. By this everyone will know that you are my disciples, if you have love for one another" (John 13:34-35). For humans, to love each other as Jesus loved is a beautiful but usually unattainable ideal. Paul's first letter to the Christian community in the Greek city of Corinth offers this more practical, but equally memorable wisdom: "Love is patient; love is kind. . . . It bears all things, believes all things, hopes all things, endures all things. Love never ends" (1 Corinthians 13:4-8a).

Our tradition also teaches that God loves us, and indeed that God is Love. The faithful love of God is etched into every page of the Bible. Even so, it is very difficult for a person to accept that teaching if the person's life is marred by neglect, violence, and abuse. The second section of this book will discuss how people can find the loving hand of God even in the turmoil and tragedy of life. In this chapter we are considering the human interactions that are indispensable elements of our quest for wholeness.

Unconditional love is precious; it is also rare. If you perceive that you are loved unconditionally, you should not take it for granted. Appreciate it, and express your appreciation often to your beloved.

In the remaining pages of this chapter we will speak of the importance of love for people of all ages—and of the dangers of forgetting to express and appreciate love.

Young Children

The most worthy recipient of unconditional love is surely a newborn baby. Most parents welcome their children in a spirit of profound love and hope. Parents will do anything for their child. They want to protect and support that child, whatever happens. Mother and father both look on their child as someone who deserves to be loved, to be cared for. Parents always wonder what will become of their child in life, and always they hope for the best. They know that love is indispensable for the present and future happiness of their child.

Even so, because of circumstances faced by their parents, some babies are born unwanted or barely tolerated. The chances of their ever growing to wholeness are limited from the outset.

Even children who are born into a loving environment sometimes suffer from deprivation before they have lived many months. Many babies cry a lot; babies demand attention and make their demands known in ways that try any parent's patience. At the same time, parents' energy is often consumed by adult preoccupations, interests, and tensions. Problems might arise from an unhappy relationship between the parents; sometimes one or even both parents never accept responsibility for the child, never offer the love the child needs. When a mother or father suffers from depression in the weeks following the birth of a child, the child may instinctively experience a deficit in the required emotional attachment unless the other parent makes up for the shortfall.

Love deficiency for young children is sometimes the result of fears related to money in a society that advertises luxury but rewards primarily those who are clever, industrious, and entrepreneurial. The problem might arise from exhaustion, as both parents must work long hours to preserve even a modest lifestyle and now have a child to care for in addition. Or the problem might be "success," as parents who have been eager participants in the marketplace want to continue enjoying the adult leisure activities to which they have become accustomed.

Young children sometimes grow up feeling that their parents consider them a nuisance. The parents "have no time" for their child. They are more involved in other issues than wiping runny noses or marveling at butterflies. When such children instinctively try to attract attention, their behavior begins to be described as problematic or uncontrollable. What they really want is love.

One of the resultant problems in schools, surprisingly, is violence in kindergarten. Many people react with incredulity to that assertion, but these are the children who are using foul language, hitting and biting other children, throwing sand or heavier classroom objects, and kicking teachers. That is violence. It is less lethal than violence in high school, but it presages later escalation. Some parents come with their children on the first day of kindergarten and say to the teacher: "I hope you can do something with him, because we can't control him." Sometimes parents of young children describe emotionally-charged conflicts with each other and then express surprise that their child has been suspended from school for behavioral offenses in kindergarten. Shockingly often, adults express regret that they ever decided to become parents. Many children feel inadequately loved in their first three or four years of life. No one should be surprised when children living in such situations explode into violent behavior at an early age, and as adults endure lives characterized by cruelty and abuse.

First and most important, children need to be accepted and loved unconditionally. Young children need to know in their hearts that they are loved, *no matter what they do.* This is by no means to say that they should be allowed to do anything they want. Such wanton permissiveness is an indication of neglect rather than love. Good discipline is defined as "setting limits with love." There will be more comment on this issue in the chapter on freedom as an element of wholeness.

It is essential that children feel a strong sense of being loved in their families; if they do not, the damage to their personalities may be almost irreparable.

Adolescents

As young people mature they seek love and affirmation from people their own age even more than from their parents. Adolescents often agree that they act like different people when they are among their friends than when they are with their families. Some parents are offended that their school-age children care more about their friends than they seem to care about their parents' approval. This, however, is the reality of growing up.

Life at home still continues to play a large part in teenagers' self-understanding, not always for the best. Sadly, high school students have been heard wistfully declaring, "I don't know whether my parents love me or not." They report that life at home is characterized by repeated demands and constant criticism, and sometimes by threats of physical violence or ejection from the home. When students say, "my father would kill me if I got pregnant" (and their mothers at meetings of parents report the same fear, using the same words), they are expressing a depth of apprehension that should not be dismissed. The result of such repeated utterances is an atmosphere in which it is very difficult for parents or children to express the unconditional love all people need.

Many are the adults who report that their parents, and especially their fathers, never expressed love for them in words. Many of these now grown offspring continue to be resentful toward one or both parents, especially if there was seriously harmful behavior associated with their upbringing. Many express the desire to do a better job of parenting than their parents did for them, but a great many young parents nonetheless continue the patterns they observed in their homes when they were children.

Other adults declare that they know their parents loved them, though the words were never spoken. "Actions speak louder than words. I know that my father loved me by the way he related to me all through my childhood." Those are the words of wise and fortunate people—but in current generations, it is still best if parents can make explicit, in words spoken to their children, the love that they believe their actions display.

Most parents would probably insist that they really do love their children deeply, despite the preoccupations and the criticism, despite their failure to express love in word and action, and even at times despite their frank dislike of the 'kind of person' their child seems to be. Some parents are even described by teachers as too supportive of their children, refusing to accept consequences for misbehavior, accusing teachers of unfairness, rejecting demands for responsible self-discipline. More will be said about this tension later, particularly in the chapter on freedom. The point of this chapter is simply that parents' deep underlying love must be expressed in word and action, repeatedly and endlessly, so that it becomes the dominant and obvious basis of their relationship with their children.

At the same time, young people should be encouraged to recognize their parents' love and good intentions and to accept responsibility for their behavior. It is not easy to ask a child to reverse a custom and express love for a parent, but parents who express their love in word and deed deserve to hear "I love you too" from their children. All of us need to know that we are loved, *no matter what we do*. No one can grow toward wholeness without feeling loved.

Adults

Adults, too, need to feel loved, and we need to express our love for the significant people in our lives repeatedly. Think about your own personal network of love. Appreciate the importance of love in your life, and express your love to the people who love you, often.

Unconditional love, though, is rare and precious. Many people in our society are motivated more by self-interest than by self-giving. The fact that so many relationships and marriages do not stand the test of time is a function of people's instinctive preference for their own concerns over the needs of their loved ones—who, usually, are equally devoted to taking care of themselves. People hurt each other in so many ways; sometimes the offenses are perceived literally as unforgivable. Unconditional love is most clearly tested and most clearly expressed in situations where forgiveness is required. "Will you continue to love this person, for better or for worse, no matter what happens?" Many who have been married for some years would no longer answer in the affirmative.

Is unconditional love possible? I believe that it is. If you are in a situation of being loved unconditionally, be glad and thankful. Never take it for granted. If you are so blessed, most likely you do express your love often, in words and in action. If you have neglected daily opportunities to express your love for everyone in your household, take advantage of this moment of awareness and speak your love aloud.

Jesus urged us to build our quest for wholeness on the cornerstone of self-giving love and forgiveness. We will discuss his wisdom in more detail in the chapter about a consistent personal value system. The brilliant paradoxical insight of the Gospel is that we can best become ourselves by giving ourselves in love. Jesus' ministry and his death were examples in action of what he preached. His exhortation to generous lifelong love is truly radical, truly countercultural in our society. "Just as I have loved you, you also should love one another" (John 13:35). In spite of the scorn of the modern marketplace, Jesus was right. Loving well, and knowing you are loved, are essential elements of human wholeness.

Reflection Questions

Each chapter will conclude with a series of questions. They can be used for personal reflection about the content of the chapter or for discussion with companions on the journey toward wholeness.

1. How would you describe the wholeness to which you aspire as a goal of life's journey? (Make your answer as wide-ranging as possible.)

2. Discuss the importance of expressing love, both in word and in action, to young children, adolescents, and adults whom we love.

3. Under what circumstances can parents' attempts to express love for their children be counterproductive?

4. What are the obstacles that prevent people from saying "I love you" right out loud? How can such obstacles be overcome?

5. Express the role of God, if any, in your personal efforts to be more loving in word and deed.

More reflection on the importance of love will be found in chapter 3, "A Consistent Personal Value System."

Chapter Two

A Sense of Purpose

Blessed are the pure in heart, for they shall see God.
(Matthew 5:8)

In this society of ours, everyone is unbelievably busy. We are endlessly active. We face demands on our time from all directions—at work, at home, at play, and in the many communities we belong to. It seems we never have a moment to phone our sister, let alone to think about the meaning of life. We hit the floor running early Monday morning, and we keep running till we fall into bed the following Sunday night.

Students may be the busiest of all, burdened by demands from parents, school, each other, sometimes the workplace, and from within themselves. Cell phones have added to their busyness; there is nowhere they can be alone if they are carrying a phone; they can have conversations with their friends by voice, text, or video, no matter where they may be. When students come home from school they immediately turn on the television or rush to the computer to visit favorite sites or play video games. Some do their homework to the tune of background sound that is often overwhelming, at least for their elders. Teenagers are renowned for being introspective, but it seems that today such reflection is done in the course of multitasking.

What everyone needs in this maelstrom of experiences is not only a moment's peace but also an all-embracing sense of purpose. The beatitude quoted at the beginning of this chapter is not about sexuality, but about singleness of purpose: to be pure in heart means to be single-minded, to know who you are and where you are going in life, and to set your priorities accordingly. The beatitude promises that those who live with purpose will "see God"—will perceive the active presence of God in their lives.

For true wholeness, all of us need to be able to identify a center in our lives, a focus, a sense of what pulls all our experiences together and gives them meaning. This is what faith is supposed to offer people: a sense of purpose, an inner peace, an understanding that everything we do (even in the most constrained circumstances) has meaning as part of our quest for wholeness.

Faith

Faith is our intuitive sense of the central purpose of our lives.

Faith is instinctive in most believers. If necessary, people may be able to articulate a credible rationale for believing, but for most people faith is a gut feeling.

This is not to disregard the importance of the cognitive side of religious experience or to disparage the value or legitimacy of believing and searching for understanding. But faith is essentially a way of life, and it has to be emotional and intuitive to be complete. A sociological survey reported in newspapers in 2007 claimed to show that a majority of believers think their own faith is rational, but the faith of others is emotional—and they think emotional faith is inadequate. On the contrary, faith that does not respond to people's deeply-felt emotional yearnings is inadequate. As we shall see in the chapter on emotional fulfillment, feelings are an essential part of wholeness.

What *is* life all about? Where can we find a central focus for our multiple activities? For many people, especially those living in happy families, love provides the unifying principle for everything they do. Others might say that life is all about their quest to be true to themselves, to be fulfilled, or to be the best person they can be. People who have a strong religious consciousness might say that they are devoting their lives to being faithful disciples of Jesus or faithful children of God. Some might say the main purpose of their lives is to go to heaven after death.

Financial Success

On a more observable level the central motivating factor in the activities of many people in our society is financial success. The prevailing religion in Western society is capitalism. When parents are asked why they want their children to get a good education, not many of them respond: "so that they will grow up to be kind and loving adults." Parents do hope that the schools instill responsible attitudes in their children, but most importantly, parents want schools to prepare students for success in the economic sphere. "What's wrong with that?" many ask when challenged. What is wrong with it is only the place it may be given in one's order of priorities. Financial success is not worthy of being called the central purpose of human life, but for many people it has become in practice more important than love or personal fulfillment or faithfulness to God.

When hardship like the economic downturn of 2008–2009 overwhelms society, the dominant sense of purpose in people's lives is seriously challenged. Workers who have offered ministry in destitute societies often tell us that poor people have a better understanding of the importance of love than most people in more comfortable societies. The destruction wrought in people's lives by economic deprivation is real. It is also an opportunity for redirection of priorities.

Most students are also enthusiastic participants in the marketplace. Children of prosperous families expect to live their lives in prosperity; their parents sometimes decry their "sense of entitlement"—their expectation that they deserve to begin their careers in the world of work at the same level of comfort their parents have achieved after decades of toil. Children of poorer families are dedicated to acquiring the lifestyle they see depicted in the media. When they do not succeed in school they sometimes pursue wealth by means that are considered unacceptable by more affluent people.

When I ask young people what they perceive to be the most important priority in the lives of adults they know, students frequently respond with a single word: money.

Almost by definition, a student is someone who is searching for meaning. Most young people build their personal sense of purpose by following the model they see in the lives of significant adults. Some students are perfectly at home in this money-dominated society, "totally sucked in" by the lure of wealth and power. On the other hand, some realize that the conventional wisdom of the marketplace is shallow and ultimately worthless. But all of them realize that it is not what adults *say* that shows what is really important in their lives; it is what they *do*.

Reassess and Reaffirm Priorities

Any of the factors mentioned in previous paragraphs—love, personal fulfillment, faithfulness to God, economic success—may contribute to a sense of purpose that gives meaning to all the many activities of our daily lives. Is it possible to choose one such factor and identify it alone as the source of *ultimate* meaning, the focus for all we do? To do so could lead to valuable resetting of priorities and a renewed feeling that we are not simply victims of our circumstances but are truly setting the course of our lives in our continuing quest for wholeness.

Whatever we identify as a source of ultimate meaning in our lives, the next step is to check our priorities in terms of the time devoted to the various factors that make up our daily lives. Western society is full of people who claim that family is the most important factor in their lives but who spend relatively little time with spouse and children. According to an unpublished sixteen-year-long study of sources of conflict between partners, "housework" and "time and attention" are the two factors that consistently cause the most conflict in couples over the long term. Rationales for partners' inadequate loving attention to each other and to their children are most often financial: we both have to work long hours just to keep ahead of our debts. Work is also a serious source of tension in our lives, and we cannot "just forget about it" when we come home. Those are all understandable reasons for domestic unrest.

Still, if the tensions between partners overflow into hostility and eventual breakdown of the relationship, children will be seriously affected by the crisis. Teachers of young children are convinced that many of the behavioral problems they meet in class are the result of issues, often financial issues, in the home. Teachers who must deal with defiant high school students often believe that the source of the students' disrespectful intensity can be traced to what was happening in their parents' lives fifteen years earlier.

This chapter is intended as an invitation to step back from the hurly-burly, to reflect about what gives meaning to your life, and to *re-affirm your sense of purpose*. This is one of the things religion can offer to believers: a chance to consider our progress and to strengthen our sense of purpose in life. In the traditional wisdom of Christianity, Lent and Advent are seasons dedicated to self-examination. In churches with a strong sacramental tradition the sacrament of forgiveness may also be used for periodic self-assessment and renewal of purpose.

Once you have reaffirmed your sense of purpose, reconsider whether your way of living is consistent with your stated priorities and decide whether changes need to be made for the ultimate good of both yourself and the people you love. A more detailed self-examination may be based on the material in the following chapters about the importance of living according to a consistent personal system of values, about freedom, and about emotional well-being.

Reconsideration of priorities and reaffirmation of purpose are often described in religious language as "continuing conversion." In biblical language, they are the content of the challenging beatitude: "Blessed are the pure in heart."

Reflection Questions

1. What does success mean to you?

2. List several factors that give meaning and purpose to your life.

3. Which of those has the highest priority? Is there one factor that unifies all the others you listed?

For personal reflection or dialogue with a close friend rather than group discussion:

- Evaluate your current way of living with regard to your stated list of priorities.

- What obstacles reduce your consistent adherence to your principles?

- What changes can be made in the next ninety days?

Chapter Three

A Consistent Personal Value System

Each of us is living according to a value system we have shaped during the course of our lives, on the basis of input from our family of origin and our friends, and indeed from our whole society. Our values may also be developed in dialogue with God, the gospels, and our faith tradition. It may seem optimistic to claim that everyone is "living according to a value system." In truth, there is great variety in personal value systems: many people, mindfully or not, seek comfort or pleasure as their primary goal; others try to acquire as many possessions as possible; still others crave the satisfaction of self-centered desires. Those, too, are value systems. The life pattern of many, perhaps, is simply to "go with the flow"—to live in a careless or irresponsible manner—but that is also a more or less conscious value system.

A value system that seeks to be Christian is exemplified by the standards proclaimed by Jesus in the gospels. Christians believe that we will find true wholeness, peace of heart, and happiness by living according to his teachings.

We are shaping our *selves* by the decisions we make, day by day. That is the moral enterprise in which every human being is engaged. To express the same idea religiously, we are building the persons we are with God's help. The action of God is entirely to support us. God reaches into our lives to lead us to wholeness, teaching us what is required of faithful believers, giving us the wisdom and courage to make good decisions, filling us with the power to love. At the end of our lives we will be the persons we (and God) have built by the choices we have made throughout our lifetime.

Many of us may "kid ourselves" as we journey through life, trying to reassure ourselves that we really are doing the best we can. Death is the "moment of truth" when the kidding stops. At death we face the truth of who we are. As suggested in the previous chapter, it is important to seek "moments of truth" periodically in the course of our lives and to reaffirm our priorities. At death the light of Truth will penetrate the depths of our hearts for the last time, and we will see ourselves as we really are. None of us will be perfect, but all of us will be more or less pleased with the person we have become. God will be present, not as a judge in a courtroom scene but as the Savior who has supported us in our quest for wholeness. There will be "no surprises." Deep in our hearts we know who we are and how we have lived, and God accepts our self-understanding. The person we have built in the course of life's journey will live forever.

In that ultimate context we are about to discuss the personal value system on which we base the decisions that shape our lives. In this chapter we will discuss a number of values that Christians consider essential components of an authentic way of life.

Moral Wisdom Radically Expressed

The moral teaching of our tradition is *wisdom*: insight about a way of life that will make us truly human, whole, civilized in the best sense, at peace, true to ourselves, and faithful to God.

The moral teachings of Jesus should be understood as wisdom rather than as law. He offers insight about how to live in a way that is truly best for us, most likely to result in wholeness and peace of heart. Jesus urged people to change their hearts, to accept the rule of God in their lives, and to grow toward wholeness in this life by living according to his teachings. God has imbued our nature with the desire to be good persons, to be fully human, and to be happy. Further, we believe that God offers spiritual energy to help us to be good, to be wise and courageous and loving. We do good because we are creatures of God, and it is both beneficial for our own well-being and appropriate for us as God's children to live according to the Gospel. Jesus taught us how to live well.

If we understand Jesus' teachings as wisdom, it is reasonable to discuss point by point whether or not his insights are valid guidance for our lives today. It is not convincing to enforce the teachings of Jesus simply on the grounds that "this is what Jesus told us to do." We do not respond well to arbitrary decrees. We want to do what is right because it is right. Thus we have to ask ourselves whether Jesus' wisdom is true. Is his teaching timeless and valid forever? Would he say the same things today to us who live in a society vastly different from his?

Surprisingly, few people in our society can list many of the moral teachings of Jesus. We have some general knowledge that he stood for integrity and love (basically, being honest and nice to each other), but few can respond in detail when asked for a list of Jesus' specific moral teachings. Further, almost all of Jesus' moral teachings are phrased in a radical form that should not usually be taken literally. We can perhaps figure out what behaviors are proposed in certain teachings, but many people feel that his teachings are so visionary as to be impractical in today's society.

Faithful believers may disagree with the preceding sentences, but see what you can recall: how many of the specific moral teachings of Jesus can you list? And how many of those should be applied literally?

One teaching that definitely can be taken literally is shared with many religious traditions around the globe: "Do to others as you would have them do to you" (Matthew 7:12). That generic teaching is valid forever, and could indeed transform society if only it were followed faithfully. Most of Jesus' moral teaching, however, is more specific than "do unto others," and his words usually express his insight with unexpected intensity.

In the following pages we will explore several of the most significant, and perhaps surprising, themes presented in the gospels as the moral wisdom of Jesus.

Number One Priority: Total Dedication to the Reign of God

> *Strive first for the kingdom of God and his righteousness.*
>
> (Matthew 6:33)

The reign of God

The term "reign [of God]" is used by many contemporary scholars in preference to "kingdom" as a translation of the original gospel word, *basileia*. (The gospels were written in Greek.) "Kingdom" is a less appropriate translation because its implications can be both political (a territory that is governed by a king) and gender-exclusive. Kings are always males. God is not male. (See the later chapter on God as Father for more discussion of that statement.)

The announcement of the coming of the reign of God was Jesus' most important teaching. Many parables begin with that phrase. Sometimes Jesus would declare that his healings demonstrated that "the kingdom of God has come to you" (Luke 11:20). Regrettably, the phrase does not resonate in the hearts of most modern believers. But it should.

"The reign of God" speaks of the sovereignty of God, God's authority, God's *influence* over a believer's life. The phrase means that if we allow God to rule in our hearts, God will transform us and lead us toward wholeness. That is the central invitation of the Gospel. The "good news" of the Bible is that, if we will consent, God will act in our lives as a spiritual force leading us toward personal fulfillment. The central question proposed to all disciples is this: "Will you let God take over in your life, transform you, and make you whole?" Jesus proclaimed that nothing else in life should matter to us as much as the reign of God.

The role of the community

The Bible understands human life primarily in regard to God's action toward us as members of the human family through the ages. Jesus' teachings are based on an understanding about human life that is very different from our modern emphasis on the value of the individual.

All through the Bible, the *community* is more important than the individual. One person's life is important only to the extent that it contributes to the entire community's welfare. People who gave their lives for the community were considered heroic; those who chose to preserve their individual lives rather than promote the common cause were regarded as cowardly. In the same vein, capital punishment was prescribed in the Law of Moses on the grounds of preserving the common good, even for such relatively minor offenses as disrespect for parents by adult children, adultery, sexual relations between men, and even gathering wood on the Sabbath (Leviticus 20:10, 13; Deuteronomy 21:18-21; Numbers 15:32). Jesus, however, seems to have been opposed to capital punishment. His intervention on behalf of the woman apprehended in the act of adultery, in the story related in John 8, is the only evidence. Nonetheless, to repeat, in the New Testament as well as in the Hebrew Scriptures, the community is of more value than the individual.

We should consider seriously the role of the community in our personal life journeys. Each of us belongs to several communities, with varying degrees of commitment: our family, our neighborhood, our workplace, our society, recreational communities, and religious communities. No one can grow to wholeness alone. Our journey is always shared with others. Belonging is an important part of wholeness. The first community in which we need to feel a sense of belonging is our family; if that community is broken, our quest is compromised—but never hopeless. We are all wounded voyagers.

Belonging to a supportive church community should be part of believers' quest for wholeness. In a church, people are supported by other members and by religious leaders. Church communities support their members by proclaiming their beliefs together, by encouraging worthy behavior, by admonishing wrongdoing, by forgiving each other, and by praying and celebrating together. It is regrettable that so many middle-aged and young people have lost a sense of belonging to a church community. Ascribing fault for this trend is unproductive, but both churches and individuals would be wise to look inward and undertake reform. For individuals, it may be valuable to realize that the family gathered around the kitchen table is a faith community and to talk explicitly about believing in that setting.

Total dedication

Jesus proclaimed the importance of single-minded dedication to the reign of God. That principle is at the root of some extremely radical directives given in Matthew's gospel: "If your right eye causes you to sin, tear it out and throw it away . . . if your right hand causes you to sin, cut it off and throw it away" (Matthew 5:29-30). Today we agree to understand such harsh sayings in a metaphorical sense rather than at face value, and we must find principled ways to live in total dedication to the reign of God in our time and in our society.

Through the ages, unfortunately, there have been people, Christian and non-Christian, who have interpreted such radical sayings quite literally. Today we think that societies that amputate the hands of thieves are barbaric, but Christian authorities have administered horribly inhumane forms of punishment against people who were considered heretics, witches, or homosexuals. War has been waged repeatedly in the name of Jesus, right up to our own time. Sacrificing one's life in defense of homeland or religious freedom has been praised through the centuries. Martyrs have been extolled in Jewish times (the Maccabees and the defenders of Masada, for example) and in Christian times. We are much less approving of contemporary martyrs who give their lives for causes with which we disagree.

In recent centuries in Western society the value of the individual person has emerged and taken precedence over the common good. Even the churches, with their emphasis on individual morality, have contributed to this development. Most contemporary Christians consider this to be a valid evolution in our principles, though we should keep in mind that the teaching of Jesus speaks of the priority of the community over the individual. Jesus challenges us to be totally dedicated to the reign of God, to be "pure of heart," to "strive first for the kingdom of God" (Matthew 6:33). What does total dedication to the reign of God involve in an age of individualism?

Relatively few people understand the meaning of their lives in terms of total dedication to the kingdom. If they could understand the connection between the reign of God and our personal quest for wholeness they might feel much more at home with Jesus' teachings. The reign of God is about God's spiritual influence in our lives. When parents give years of their lives in loving dedication to their spouse and to the upbringing of their children, they are living in total dedication to the reign of God. When members of religious communities spend their lives in the service of God's people, they are living in total dedication to the reign of God. When workers or students conscientiously perform their tasks to the best of their ability, they are living in total dedication to the reign of God.

Some outcomes of the increasing focus on the value of the individual have not been widely accepted in many circles of Christianity. One example is human rights legislation that has been adopted in many societies. Many believers and church leaders strongly disagree with legislation that gives full human rights to formerly disadvantaged groups (for example, women and gays). At times, Catholic politicians and judges are maligned by some religious leaders for voting in favor of human rights legislation.

Such laws, however, are rightly understood by some believers as being faithful to Jesus' concern for the downtrodden.

The reign of God is the result of God's saving influence in our lives. "The reign of God is within you/among you." It is both a personal and a communal reality. In the communal sense the reign of God is realized in the community of believers, all of whom are supporting each other in their quest for wholeness.

Once again, the good news of our religious tradition is that we do not have to grow toward wholeness by our own efforts. "God saves us" means "God reaches into our lives to lead us toward wholeness." If we will allow God to reign in our hearts, God will transform us and give us the strength to live in a way that is truly best for us, truly loving, truly faithful to God. Jesus teaches that we will never be able to become the best persons we can be if we rely only on our own power. We need each other, and we need God's help, day by day, to grow to wholeness. That is the good news proclaimed in the Bible; that is the meaning of the beatitude urging us to be "pure in heart," and that is the beauty of Jesus' challenge to be totally dedicated to the reign of God in our inner lives.

The Dangers of Money

> *Blessed are you who are poor, for yours is the kingdom of God . . .*
> *but woe to you who are rich, for you have received your consolation.*
> (Luke 6:20, 24)

The economic sphere is the area of greatest preoccupation for most people in our world, whether they are desperately poor, struggling, or comfortable. Jesus knew that very well, so as one might expect, economic issues are the single most important concern in the moral teaching of Jesus.

Jesus warned about the role of money in people's lives. He recognized the damage that can be wrought by the power of wealth, and he understood that anxiety about possessions becomes more important than love in many lives. Jesus told

parables about rich fools who worked endlessly to store up trea-
sures, only to die before they could enjoy them (Luke 12:13-21).
In his legendary "lilies of the field" speech he proclaimed a
"what, me worry?" attitude that would be entirely unacceptable
in today's middle-class society, if anyone ever considered its
obvious implications: "do not worry about your life, what you
will eat or what you will drink. . . . Consider the lilies of the
field, how they grow; they neither toil nor spin. . . . if God so
clothes the grass of the field . . . will he not much more clothe
you? . . . do not worry about tomorrow, for tomorrow will bring
worries of its own" (Matthew 6:25-34). No responsible partici-
pant in the contemporary marketplace could accept this teaching
of Jesus literally, nor would anyone who proclaimed such
thoughts be hired by a modern employer.

Then there are the teachings, in addition to the beatitude
quoted at the beginning of this section, that confront the dangers
of money more directly:

- "How hard it will be for those who have wealth to enter the
  kingdom of God!" (Mark 10:23)

- "It is easier for a camel to go through the eye of a needle
  than for someone who is rich to enter the kingdom of God."
  (Luke 18:25)

- "No one can serve two masters . . . You cannot serve God
  and wealth." (Matthew 6:24)

- "Give to everyone who begs from you, and do not refuse
  anyone who wants to borrow from you." (Matthew 5:42)

- "If you lend to those from whom you hope to receive, what
  credit is that to you? . . . But love your enemies, do good,
  and lend, expecting nothing in return." (Luke 6:34-35)

- "None of you can become my disciple if you do not give
  up all your possessions." (Luke 14:33)

Pope Benedict XVI has written that such sayings of Jesus "terrify us."[1] In Jesus' society the vast majority of people were poor and suffered oppression at the hands of a few who were wealthy and powerful. Still today, a majority of the world's people—as well as a minority in Western society—are poor and suffer oppression at the hands of the economically fortunate. We in the middle class must recognize that Jesus was warning *us*. We are the rich people of our world. Since Jesus stood with the poor and against the rich who dominated and oppressed them, Jesus stands against us with regard to the economic aspect of our lives.

Most middle-class believers are convinced that those teachings of Jesus cannot be taken literally. Many, both adults and students, actually argue with Jesus in discussions and give reasons why his teachings are mistaken, or do not apply to us. They may be right in saying that the words cannot be taken literally by every believer. It would not benefit us or others if we sold everything we own and gave the money away.

Even the author of Matthew's gospel recognized that Jesus' beatitude about poverty was stated in an extreme way. (Most scholars consider that its original form is found in Luke 6:20 and 24: "Blessed are you who are poor . . . but woe to you who are rich." Jesus is speaking to those who have little money and to those who have more than enough.) Matthew expressed what he considered to be the essential meaning of the beatitude by amending it to "Blessed are the poor in spirit," a phrase that seems more compatible with a comfortable lifestyle. Still we must face the crucial question: How can we apply the challenging wisdom of Jesus' teachings about money to our lives as responsible citizens of Western society?

The radical sayings of Jesus about the dangers of money pose a major challenge for us who wish to be faithful disciples of Jesus but prefer to live comfortably in the middle class. Was Jesus right

[1] Pope Benedict XVI, *Jesus of Nazareth*, large print ed. (New York: Random House, 2007), 180 (near the end of the section on the beatitudes).

when he taught that the pursuit of money is extremely dangerous to our search for wholeness? Was he right in thinking that
people who are devoted to acquiring things tend to forget the
demands of love? Would he still say that the worst thing that
could happen to our children is that they grow up to be rich?!!
Would he berate us faithful churchgoers about our level of consumption that consigns millions of families around the world
to abject poverty and is destroying our planet's ecosystems at
the same time? There is no doubt.

What must I do to apply the radically-stated wisdom of Jesus
to my life? At the very least I must understand my possessions
primarily as opportunities to serve *others*. My actions must show
that love is more important to me than money. The preceding
sentences are far too gentle, but they do offer possible criteria
for critical analysis of my lifestyle: can my family and friends
consistently see in my behavior that I use a significant portion
of my possessions in the service of others? Does love have a
higher priority than money in my actions, and not just in my
words?

When we discuss specific contemporary situations, many
believers will disagree about the implications of those general
principles. Few adults think of the size of their mortgage as
impairing their dedication to the reign of God or their personal
quest for wholeness. Yet many upwardly-mobile urban couples
have bought houses at staggering costs, with the result that both
partners have to work long hours to serve their mortgage and
credit card debts; they are often overwhelmed by the tensions
involved in their adult lives; they have little time to devote to
each other and to their children; their tension-driven actions
may cause serious hostility within their family. Sometimes they
perceive themselves as victims, especially when the economy
reduces the value of their homes to less than the outstanding
principal on their mortgage. The pursuit of wealth may be hin-
dering their personal growth, but they may never realize that
their decision about the size of their mortgage was indeed a
moral choice that might have been predicted to have a harmful

effect on their journey toward true wholeness. The wisdom of Jesus about the dangers of wealth is being proven true in such people's lives.

Another application is related to the ongoing destruction of our planet's ecosystems. Many people in our northern-hemisphere society can afford to enjoy asparagus in February, though it must be imported from faraway places at that time of year. We would rather not be asked to consider what effect international agribusiness is having on the ecosystems of the exporting countries, or how many of the workers are children, or how well the farm workers are paid. Nor do we wish to hear that the transportation of such produce injects carbon into the atmosphere that is more than the weight of the product itself. (Every long airplane trip we take does the same: more than the weight of each passenger is deposited into the air as carbon emissions.)[2] Many of us prefer to buy heavy automobiles with large engines because we enjoy their power and because they are "safer"—but they are not safer, not for the welfare of this planet and not for the person in a smaller car that collides with such a vehicle. Our relentless consumption is harming others and crippling our planet.

If I am to live in the spirit of Jesus I must see my possessions primarily as opportunities to serve the needs of others. I must continually ask myself whether I am generous enough in sharing my wealth with poor and suffering people, close to home and around the world. Would I prefer instead, like the rich man in one of Jesus' challenging parables (Luke 16:19-31), to get the beggars off the streets so I do not have to step around them on my way to work or to the theater? The standard proclaimed by Jesus is expressed in the classic statement, "I was hungry and you gave me food . . ." (Matthew 25:35).

---

[2] George Radnoti, *Profit Strategies for Air Transportation* (New York: McGraw-Hill Professional, 2002), 202. The chapter about the many factors that are considered with regard to fuel economy reports that a Boeing 747 burns 25,000 pounds of fuel per hour. At maximum payload, 65 pounds of fuel per passenger is burned each hour.

With issues like these surrounding every decision we make, we must ask ourselves what effect the teaching of Jesus should have on our economic lives. Many believers think that faith should not be considered when we make decisions about money. But Jesus talked about money a great deal. What would the world look like if Jesus were in control of world economies? A ridiculous impossibility, you may say. But am I a disciple of Jesus, or am I a child of the marketplace? No one can serve both masters, says Jesus.

Jesus was right about the dangers of money. He would say the same thing to us. And we must constantly reconsider our response to his teachings as we proceed on our journey toward wholeness.

Forgive, Resent, or Retaliate?

Jesus spoke frequently about the importance of forgiveness. In keeping with his Jewish heritage, he proclaimed God as a forgiving God. A chapter about God's forgiveness is found in the second section of this book. More significantly, Jesus connected God's forgiveness with our forgiveness of each other, saying (in his only reported comment on the Our Father), "if you forgive others their trespasses, your heavenly Father will also forgive you; but if you do not forgive others, neither will your Father forgive your trespasses" (Matthew 6:14-15).

In a chapter that has been called "the charter of the Christian community," Jesus teaches that mutual forgiveness is the indispensable glue that must hold a community together. It is in that setting (Matthew 18:21-22) that Jesus responds to Peter's request for a limit: "How often should I forgive?" Jesus' well-known response means that there is no limit: "Not seven times, but, I tell you, seventy times seven." Later in the same chapter Jesus tells a parable about a slave who is severely punished for not dismissing a small debt after his own large debt had been dismissed. "So my heavenly Father will do to every one of you, if you do not forgive your brother or sister from your heart" (Matthew 18:35).

Surely the most striking and radical statement of Jesus against retaliation in the face of offense is "if anyone strikes you on the right cheek, turn the other also" (Matthew 5:39). The teaching has become axiomatic in our culture, but it is not honored in the behavior of the majority in the Western world. Mahatma Gandhi used it as an example of teachings of Jesus that he agreed with, but observed that Christians have never accepted in practice. Moreover, few believers have reflected on the teaching that immediately precedes it: "I say to you, Do not resist an evildoer." This saying seems to go beyond "nonviolent resistance" to "nonresistance." Many adult believers would declare that both sayings of Jesus are practically impossible to follow literally in everyday life.

In conversations about these remarkable teachings many young people express their conviction that the teaching of Jesus simply cannot be practiced in our society. They believe that if you do not retaliate, the offender will abuse you again. They know the teaching of Jesus, and may even agree with it in principle, but they feel that the world they live in makes it impossible to live according to the Gospel. In fact, some years ago in a formal sociological survey about religious education, 45 percent of Catholic high school students disagreed with the statement: "Jesus is a good model for me to follow in my life."[3] They sincerely believe that the teaching of Jesus cannot be followed in our society. Jesus, they think, was divine; he could not sin. He was not like us; he did not face the problems we face. Many adult believers probably think the same, but would not express that opinion aloud.

Many of us live according to the morality of the marketplace: "An eye for an eye . . ." That is the very teaching from the Law of Moses (Exodus 21:24) that Jesus was radicalizing in his "turn the other cheek" saying: "You have heard that it was said, 'An eye for an eye and a tooth for a tooth.' But I say to you, Do not

[3] *The Blishen Report* (Toronto: Ontario Conference of Catholic Bishops, 1991). Not available as a published document.

resist an evildoer. But if anyone strikes you on the right cheek, turn the other also" (Matthew 5:38).

Would Jesus say the same thing to us, in our complex society, two thousand years later? If so, is Jesus right?

When Jesus teaches that we should not retaliate but should forgive one another, it must not be seen as some kind of arbitrary, paradoxical law. Rather, his teaching is *wisdom* about what is really best for us, what will make us most fully human. If we spend our lives taking offense at setbacks, nursing grudges, and making plans for revenge, we are going to be eaten by those inner fires. We will be angry, nasty, unhappy people. If we can bring ourselves to forgive, we will be more peaceful, more truly human, happier. Jesus' wisdom is true, and just as valid today as it was when it was first spoken.

Are we who are disciples of Jesus, therefore, to live our lives as doormats, allowing oppressors to run roughshod over us? Our challenge, rather, is to find a way to make the radically-stated wisdom of Jesus have a consistent effect in our lives. Perhaps a way of expressing it is to say that we should work to make the offender stop oppressing us, but we should not take revenge for the offense. In any case, we must forgive the offender "from the heart."

How many times do I have to forgive? We have recalled Jesus' teaching in this regard. To express the question another way, is any offense unforgivable? Most people would say yes. Few sincere believers could forgive a person who sexually or physically abused them. Few spouses can forgive partners who beat them, or terrify and abuse their children. Most of us can only marvel at the example of the Amish people in Pennsylvania who expressed forgiveness toward a man who murdered several of their children; they welcomed the remnants of his family into their community. Other newsworthy examples have been reported in recent years.

It is understandable that many people find some offenses unforgivable, but that does not make the wisdom of Jesus untrue. Their inability to forgive is not a sign that they are bad or sinful people; rather, it is a measure of the depth of the injury that was done to them. Sometimes people say: "I know I would be more at peace, if only I could forgive what was done to me—but I can't." With such phrases they are literally expressing their acceptance of the wisdom of Jesus. What was done to them has stolen the peace from their heart and reduced the wholeness they can experience or hope for in their lives. They wish they could forgive; they hope for peace. Sometimes they even pray for peace and for the ability to forgive, but peace has been taken from them.

One hopes that somehow such people can be helped to face their woundedness and to realize that the harm that was done to them is now part of their history and their self-identity. They need to go forward from here, wounded but healed and forgiving. Perhaps, if they can open their hearts to the spiritual strength God offers, they will regain momentum in their quest for wholeness.

All of us need to be forgiven at times, and all of us are more peaceful people if we can forgive.

Sex and Marriage

We have very little wisdom from Jesus about sex. He spoke often about the dangers of wealth and the value of forgiveness, but almost never about sexual values. In one well-known saying (that really cannot be called "teaching about sexuality") he infuriated his opponents, the chief priests and elders, by asserting that "the tax collectors and the prostitutes are going into the kingdom of God ahead of you" (Matthew 21:31).

Jesus gave us no wisdom about how married people can enjoy a successful sexual relationship. "Love one another as I have loved you" (John 12:34) is a useful standard for married people and for all people, but it is not primarily about sexuality, and it is so broad that practical applications must be developed for every situation. We have no recorded teaching of Jesus about sexual relationships before marriage, masturbation, contraception, homosexuality, or any other of the vexed questions that face modern believers in the realm of sexuality.

Adultery

All the reported sayings of Jesus that relate to sexuality are addressed to married people. Jesus clearly accepted the traditional teaching of the Ten Commandments against adultery (unfaithfulness in marriage), but apparently did not agree with the Law's imposition of capital punishment for adultery (John 8:1-11). Beyond that, we know nothing about what he thought about sex.

Of course, society was vastly different two thousand years ago. Because of the very high rate of childhood mortality, people married very soon after puberty and began to bear children as soon as possible, in the realization that only a small percentage of their children would grow to adulthood. Prepubertal children were not considered bound by the Law of Moses, so all regulations about sexuality are addressed to adults, and therefore primarily to married people.

In Jesus' society, wives were considered the property of their husbands, and the adultery law was used to protect husbands' rights. The adultery commandment was interpreted as a law against "wife-stealing"—a married man who had intercourse with an unmarried woman was not considered guilty of adultery. Any man who had intercourse with a married woman was guilty of adultery (stealing the other man's wife), and the punishment was death for both parties.

We do have a record of two types of sayings of Jesus with regard to the sexual area of human life. Both of them should be recognized, like the other moral teachings of Jesus, as radical and idealistic expressions. The challenge for intelligent Christians now is to perceive the wisdom in the sayings and apply them faithfully to contemporary life.

LOOK AT A WOMAN WITH LUST . . .

> "You have heard that it was said, 'You shall not commit adultery.' But I say to you that everyone who looks at a woman with lust has already committed adultery with her in his heart." (Matthew 5:27-28)

In essence this saying of Jesus applies to all of life, not only to the area of sexuality. It proclaims the profound wisdom that all morality is primarily a matter of intention. Deeds must be evaluated, but the crucial factor in our decision making is within us. The challenge to all Christians is to bring our minds and hearts into accord with truth, and then act in a way we know will keep us growing toward wholeness. Our deeds are only symptoms of our intentions.

This insight of Jesus, though not without precedent in Jewish tradition, is a great step forward in understanding human behavior. In many ways his wisdom has still not been accepted, since popular understanding of morality focuses almost exclusively on deeds and declares certain actions as *automatically* sinful without reference to conscience or intention. We will discuss the meaning of sin more fully in the chapter on the forgiving nature of God.

Through the Christian centuries the saying of Jesus has usually been interpreted as applying only to the realm of sexuality, and has been broadened, perhaps justifiably, beyond the area of adultery to apply to every aspect of sexual life. In an era when the average interval between puberty and marriage is expanding toward twenty years we should reflect carefully on the wisdom and implications of the teaching of Jesus. It must be understood in contemporary society to mean something much different from what many of us heard in our youth: that any sexual thought, feeling, fantasy, or pleasure experienced by unmarried people is a temptation to sin.

In the first place, the saying is literally addressed only to married people. It refers specifically to *adultery*, which means unfaithfulness to the marriage bond. (We will briefly mention that it is addressed only to *men* and their attitude toward women.) Let us agree that the saying should be understood as applying to both women and men, that it is relevant to all human sexual experience (not just adultery), and that the central point of the teaching is that in all areas of human activity the intention is more important than the deed.

Second, the saying speaks of lust. In twenty-first-century Western society "lust" means little more than sexual interest. Sexual interest is considered acceptable in society, and permeates every area of public life, especially advertising and entertainment. That is not necessarily a bad thing. The Bible itself was quite forthright about sex and its place in human life: it was aware of the harm people could do to each other in the realm of sexuality, but it recognized the beauty and importance of sex and it even used sexual imagery in portraying the relationship between God and humanity. We are sexual beings, and sexual interest is part of who we are.

The word "lust" in the teaching of Jesus quoted above, however, does not refer to simple sexual interest; it is about *oppressive* sexual intention. Some years ago Pope John Paul II asserted that it is possible for a husband to offend against his own wife by "looking at her with lust." The Western world was incredulous, thinking that the pope was forbidding husbands to have sexual desire even toward their own wives. But the pope was talking about the real meaning of lust: the desire to oppress a person sexually, to impose sexual activity without regard for the wishes of one's partner. Husbands can indeed oppress their wives sexually; people in general too often behave oppressively toward each other in the realm of sexuality. Jesus' insightful teaching is that even the intention to oppress a person sexually is already harmful.

How should we express the broader wisdom in this teaching of Jesus? Morality is indeed a matter of intention. To form a firm intention to do harm to anyone, in any area of life, is already to do evil. Actually doing the deed *adds* to the evil.

In our quest for wholeness, the challenge for us believers is to bring our hearts and minds into tune with what is really best, and then to act out of that realization. This teaching of Jesus is not a condemnation of fantasy or wishing, or indeed of giving thought to temptation. We will always be tempted to do what is less than our best. Jesus himself was tempted to be the wrong kind of Messiah—to be the political leader everyone was expecting in his time. He decided to do what he knew was best. We often choose to do what we know is *less* than the best we could do: we are not totally dedicated to living according to the reign of God. The saying of Jesus reminds us that it is wrong to form a firm intention to do harm to others, in the realm of sexuality or any other aspect of our lives. The wisdom of Jesus is a guide for our intentions: always remember the goal of true wholeness. His challenge to us is to figure out what is the best thing to do in every situation—and then to do it.

THE DIVORCE SAYINGS

The other teaching of Jesus that is related to sexuality is his declaration opposing men's right to divorce their wives—a privilege men in his culture could not imagine living without. (See Matthew 19:10.) In Jewish tradition a man was permitted to divorce his wife if he "found something shameful in her." Interpreters discussed what behaviors could be considered "shameful" and therefore grounds for divorce. One respected opinion was that it was up to the husband to decide whether his wife's actions merited termination of the marriage.

The well-known sayings appear in the context of a dialogue with Pharisees and disciples in Matthew 19. (Similar sayings can also be found in Matthew 5:32, and in Mark and Luke.) In that setting Jesus refers to the original intention of God in the story of Adam and Eve, and declares that the permission to divorce that was granted in the Law of Moses was a temporary concession, because "you were so hard-hearted."

What God has joined together, let no one separate. (Matthew 19:6)

"Whoever divorces his wife, except for unchastity, and marries another commits adultery." His disciples said to him, "If such is the case of a man with his wife, it is better not to marry." (Matthew 19:9-10)

The lasting wisdom in this teaching of Jesus is that at its best, in the original intention of God, marriage lasts for the life of the partners.

In a society where women were unable to divorce oppressive or unfaithful husbands, and men were permitted to divorce their wives for any reason they found "shameful" (Deuteronomy 24:1), the teaching of Jesus was clearly of greatest benefit to women in his time. In Christian society, says Jesus, no man should have such power that he can dismiss his wife from the family for any reason he considers good enough.

By the way, long dissertations have been written about the "exception clause" ("except for unchastity") in the divorce saying in Matthew's gospel. Since it is found only in Matthew, and not in the identical sayings reported in Mark and Luke, most commentators agree that it was not part of Jesus' original teaching, but was added by the community in which Matthew's gospel developed. It seems clear that the word in Matthew's exception clause that is translated "unchastity" (*porneia* in Greek—the root of our word pornography) does not mean "adultery"; the word for adultery (*moichea*) appears later in the same saying. In Jewish society the penalty for adultery was not divorce, but death. What kind of unchastity was understood to be acceptable grounds for divorce in Matthew's community is not clear. Still, the original saying of Jesus himself included no such exception and was, as usual, radical and idealistic. Matthew's community apparently felt free to propose an exception ("unchastity"). Thirty years before Matthew's gospel was written, the great early missionary Paul applied Jesus' teaching to situations in the community of Corinth (see 1 Corinthians 7:12-16) and also proposed an exception to the idealistic proclamation of Jesus against divorce.

How can believers best adapt New Testament wisdom to contemporary married life? Most accept the insight that marriage at its best will last for life. But what should the individual and the community do when a marriage, for whatever constellation of reasons, is oppressive for one or both parties, and harmful to their quest for wholeness? Most believers today do not think that Jesus would insist that a couple stay together though they are constantly arguing, hurting each other, and distressing their children. No doubt he would urge the partners to grow in peace, but often the relationship has deteriorated so much that a peaceful relationship has become impossible. This is not to say that Jesus would accept unfaithfulness, or one partner leaving another because a seemingly more attractive relationship has developed. Even in such cases, though, we must consider Jesus' repeated wisdom about the value of forgiveness.

Most observers of contemporary society are concerned about rising divorce rates. Sociologists explore the factors that are causing this unrest in society. One important factor is the increasing economic independence of women—very much a good thing—with the result that women are no longer forced to remain in oppressive situations. Another factor seems to be self-interest: many people in our society have been brought up to expect that when they marry, their needs and wants will be met in their home. When people enter marriage with that expectation, they often fail to recognize and serve the needs of their partners. Soon they come to the realization that marriage involves self-giving and perseverance, and often they are unwilling to modify their expectations and behavior enough to bring peace to the partnership. All observers agree that the children of a partnership are seriously harmed by discord in the home and by the separation of their parents.

Obviously the efforts of the believing community must be to help people to form strong, lasting, mutually beneficial relationships, so that married life will not so often be the major disappointment it seems to be for many married people. This is not an easy goal, especially since it must involve promoting values that are countercultural in this society dominated by the marketplace and the media—in particular, the value of self-giving love and the dangers of selfishness. Still, we believers must help each other form better relationships.

Also, the believing community must find nonjudgmental ways to support partners and children who have suffered through marriage breakdown. In time most partners look for new relationships, and the community must again try to help them form strong relationships on the basis of self-giving love. The divorce rate is higher among those who have remarried, so clearly some partners are not doing well at learning from past failures. Children are most vulnerable, and often most distressed as new relationships develop. We have to find better ways to support them, despite many young people's tendency to suffer alone and to express their pain by anger and misbehavior. Perhaps the best resource the believing community could offer would be provided by people who have lived through this heartbreaking situation and have found happiness and wholeness for both partners and children in a new marriage.

In struggling with the formidable problem of divorce and remarriage among people who want to be faithful to the Gospel, it is important to recall the basic principles of this chapter and this book: that everyone's life of faith is a quest for wholeness, and that the moral wisdom of Jesus is always expressed in radical and visionary language. When people have been unable to achieve the ideal of a lifelong marriage, believers should support them in their grief, remind them of the forgiving nature of God, and assist them, where so desired, to form new relationships and to try again to achieve Jesus' ideal: lifelong marriage.

Honesty

> ". . . you have heard that it was said to those of ancient times,
> 'You shall not swear falsely . . .'
> But I say to you, Do not swear at all . . .
> Say 'yes' when you mean 'yes,' and 'no' when you mean 'no';[4]
> anything more than this comes from the evil one."
>
> (Matthew 5:37; see also James 5:12)

[4] Author's paraphrase.

The second half of chapter 5 in the Gospel according to Matthew presents six "antitheses" (contrasts) in which Jesus is reported to have drawn a distinction between teachings from the Law of Moses and his own more radical insights. In the opening phrase of the passage quoted above he may be referring to the well-known commandment, "You shall not bear false witness against your neighbor." (Exodus 20:16; Deuteronomy 5:20) That law prohibited perjury—lying under oath as a witness in court.

Some rabbis were opposed to all oath-taking, since they considered oaths to be violations of the commandment that prohibited "taking God's name in vain." In the same spirit, in the teaching quoted at the beginning of this section, Jesus declared that his disciples should never take an oath at all. He considered it irreverent to bring God into courtroom disputes as the ultimate support for someone's testimony. In his customary radical style, Jesus describes oaths as coming "from the evil one." Like any good Jew he certainly would have objected to our contemporary careless use of God's name. ("Oh my God!" "I swear to God.")

Jesus' prohibition of oaths has been ignored by most Christian communities through the centuries. Courts and churches recognize that (as with all moral teachings of Jesus) Jesus' prohibition of oaths is an idealistic teaching expressed in a radical form, and they have continued to make use of oaths. No doubt we will trust people to tell the truth when the reign of God comes in its fullness, but in the interim, society sometimes requires people to invoke God in support of their credibility. A very few Christian denominations (Quakers and Mennonites) have accepted Jesus' teaching literally and refused to take oaths, even under threat of persecution. Perhaps as a result they are considered to be among the most trustworthy of citizens. In recent years, primarily as a result of respect for cultures whose Scriptures are other than the Bible, courts have begun to accept solemn affirmations of truthfulness rather than oaths.

The main point of this section of the gospel, however, is not about Jesus' prohibition of oaths. It is about the positive side of Jesus' teaching. Disciples of Jesus should simply tell the truth because it is true. "Say 'yes' when you mean 'yes.'" The moral wisdom of Jesus is that honesty is a very important component of human wholeness and an indispensable element of human relationships. The teaching is significant enough to be included among the important moral issues dealt with in the six antitheses in Matthew 5:20-48.

Later in Matthew's gospel Jesus is reported to have said: "On the day of judgment you will have to give an account for every careless word you utter; for by your words you will be justified, and by your words you will be condemned" (Matthew 12:36). Radically expressed as always, the teaching inspires a meditation on the power of words. Words can change people's lives for good or ill. Praise evokes greater accomplishment; expressions of love transform the beloved. Reputation is an important part of a person's identity; unjustly maligning people does irreparable damage. Lies destroy relationships, even before the lies are discovered. Cheating on employers or taxing authorities involves costs that can cripple a company or an economy.

My faithful disciples, says Jesus, are honest people. They know that every careless word has power. They say "yes" when they mean "yes."

Self-giving Love

"I give you a new commandment, that you love one another.
Just as I have loved you, you also should love one another.
By this everyone will know that you are my disciples,
   if you have love for one another."

                                                    (John 13:34-35)

Jesus' wisdom about the importance of love is doubtless the best known of his moral insights. In Matthew, Mark, and Luke, Jesus agrees with a traditional Jewish opinion in identifying "you shall love your neighbor as yourself" (Leviticus 19:18) as the second most important of the laws of Moses, after "You shall love the LORD your God with all your heart, and with all your soul, and with all your might" (Deuteronomy 6:5).

After he identifies love of neighbor as one of the greatest commandments, Jesus is immediately asked: "who is my neighbor?" That question had been debated by Jewish scholars for centuries; a common opinion was that only members of the Jewish people qualified as "neighbors" under the Law. Jesus responds to the question by telling the parable of the Good Samaritan (Luke 10:29-37), a story that exhorts disciples to love even people for whom they feel hostility. His hearers' attitude to Samaritans was comparable to the mutual attitude of Israelis and Palestinians today. "Which of these three, do you think, was a *neighbor* to the man who fell into the hands of the robbers?" asks Jesus at the end of the parable. "He said, 'The one who showed him mercy.' Jesus said to him, 'Go and do likewise.'"

Another passage offers similar wisdom: "Love your enemies, do good to those who hate you. . . . If you love those who love you, what credit is that to you?" (Luke 6:27, 32; Matthew 5:43-47). Jesus' admonition that we are to love even our enemies is truly shocking, and as a result is customarily ignored by many believers at both the personal and public levels. We seem to feel that it is acceptable to proclaim Jesus' wisdom to school-age children—but they are not the ones who have lasting enemies. Many adults can identify certain people in their lives as enemies. Thinking of what those enemies have done disrupts our peace of heart; often we feel that it is impossible to overcome our long-lasting feelings of resentment. Jesus, however, would advise us to rise above the resentment and love our enemies. One Christian teacher who had been brought up as a Buddhist offered this interpretation: Jesus challenges us to do good things repeatedly for people whom we identify as our enemies, until they realize that they have no reason to be our enemies any longer.

More than a century ago, Friedrich Nietzsche called Jesus' teaching harmful, referring to it as a morality of resentment.[5] He perceived Christian teaching as the attempt of incompetent

---

[5] See the discussion in Benedict XVI, *Jesus of Nazareth* (large print edition), 182–83.

failures to vilify people who are strong and successful, and recommended building our lives on unscrupulous self-interest. The principles of Nietzsche have obviously been put into practice by many, including some nominally Christian people, in modern society. We who profess to be followers of Jesus must at least face the question: which philosophy of life is more true? Will happiness best be found on the basis of self-interest or of self-giving love? Each of us must consider this fundamental question, decide, and then make whatever changes are needed in our lives to be faithful to the principles we assert.

In John's gospel the three sentences quoted at the beginning of this section sum up Jesus' central teaching on love. The Law of Moses required love of neighbor as we love ourselves, but Jesus presents *his own life* as the model for disciples: we are to love each other as he has loved us—a shockingly radical teaching when we consider the results of his self-giving love. He goes on to say that mutual love will be the hallmark of the community of disciples; this is how everyone will know that we are his disciples. When people look at the lives of us who call ourselves followers of Jesus, do they remark, "Those Christians must really have something! Have you noticed how they love each other?" Let us hope that people do notice, and let us continue to seek to build our lives, in our families and workplaces, on the foundation of self-giving love. For love, given and received, is an indispensable element of human wholeness.

It is regrettable that, beyond the generic principles, Jesus gave us no further details about how to live in love every day. Some guidance can be found in the middle paragraph of Paul's famous chapter on love in the first letter to the Corinthians (see below), and also in Colossians 3:12-15. Those passages are often used as part of wedding ceremonies. Society would be far more peaceful if married couples were able to build their lives less on the principle of self-interest that characterizes our society and more on the Christian principle of self-giving love.

Beyond the few practical sentences reproduced below, Christian believers are reduced to the trial-and-error method as they seek to discover how to live each day in self-giving love. Every generation must learn to love all over again. The effort really does deserve more reflection, more discussion, and more time than most adults give it.

> As God's chosen ones, holy and beloved, clothe yourselves with compassion, kindness, humility, meekness, and patience. Bear with one another and, if anyone has a complaint against another, forgive each other. . . . Above all, clothe yourselves with love, which binds everything together in perfect harmony. And let the peace of Christ rule in your hearts. (Colossians 3:12-15)

> Love is patient; love is kind; love is not envious or boastful or arrogant or rude. It does not insist on its own way; it is not irritable or resentful; it does not rejoice in wrongdoing, but rejoices in the truth. It bears all things, believes all things, hopes all things, endures all things. Love never ends. (1 Corinthians 13:4-8)

> This is my prayer: that your love may abound more and more, both in wisdom and depth of experience, to help you to determine what is truly best. (Philippians 1:9-10)[6]

The Role of the Community

No one can grow to wholeness alone. Our journey is always shared with others. All of us, and especially our children, are forming and revising our personal value systems as we confront the joys and sorrows of life.

For one who is in the process of forming a personal value system, the church can function as a support community. The church is a community of people who are trying to live the Gospel in their daily lives, and who need the strength that comes from the example and the considered opinions of other believers, particularly of church leaders. Some members of the community

[6] Author's paraphrase.

will be supported by seeing what we value (and they see our values much more clearly in what we *do* than in what we say). Others, especially young people, want us to present our point of view with respect for their opinions; they do not want us to preach; they do not benefit from ultimatums; they do not want us to impose "guilt trips."

We will experience most success in passing on our values to our children and grandchildren if we realize that we cannot decide for them. We can guide; we can offer the wisdom of our tradition and our experience; we can model appropriate behavior, but ultimately it is the young people themselves who are forming their own consciences. Sometimes their values will be different from ours. Sometimes young people will make mistakes; sometimes they will be right and we will be wrong. We must respect their struggle and their search.

All of us need each other's help as we form our own sense of what is right. Mutual support and community reflection are indispensable to every person's struggle to establish and live by a consistent personal value system.

Conclusion: A Consistent Personal Value System

Making decisions on the basis of what is truly best is an important part of wholeness. Whatever our responsibly chosen values may be, we will recognize at "the moment of truth" that our lives have been authentic and that we have reached a good measure of wholeness if we can say that we have built our lives on a consistent personal value system.

For us believers, the values proclaimed by Jesus are true. He invariably stated them in a radical form, and the challenge for those who wish to be his disciples is to find a way to apply his wisdom in our lives. The principles of behavior discussed in this chapter are:

- Our best decisions are rooted in constant openness to God's wholeness-supporting action—another way of saying "total dedication to the reign of God."

- Money is a dominant factor in everyone's life, but we will be happier people if our actions express our awareness that love is more important than money, and that money is best used in the service of others.

- Being able to forgive and accept forgiveness is an essential component of peace of heart.

- Successful marriages are built on self-giving love and faithfulness. Sexual relationships must be free of any form of oppression or coercion.

- Honesty is important for us who wish to live in integrity.

- We are most truly ourselves when we give ourselves in love. Consistent self-giving love is not always easy, but it is indispensable for personal wholeness.

We must continually remind ourselves of these challenging Gospel values and reflect on their impact on our lives. Consistently living according to our values is an important component of our quest for wholeness.

Reflection Questions

1. What are the implications of understanding the moral teaching of Jesus as wisdom rather than as law?

2. Express in your own words how openness to the saving action of God and "total dedication to the reign of God" can be lived in your personal context.

3. Reflect on Jesus' teachings about the dangers of wealth. Then choose a number of contemporary economic issues, consider what Jesus would likely teach about such issues, and decide

whether his teachings in this regard are true and relevant in our time and should affect your behavior.

4. Consider the wisdom of Jesus about the importance of forgiveness. What would Jesus say about offenses most people consider unforgivable? Is Jesus' wisdom true?

5. Explore the implications of Jesus' teachings against oppression in the area of sexuality, and in favor of faithfulness in marriage.

6. What should your community of believers do to help reduce the rate of divorce in first marriages and to support people who have suffered through marriage breakdown?

7. Consider some examples of the transforming or damaging power of words and the value of honesty. If your discussion goes beyond the personal level, search for actions that can be taken by ordinary citizens to overcome the harm done by dishonesty in word and deed.

8. Are you aware of having enemies? What can you do to bring peace of heart to yourself and, if possible, to the other? Connect this discussion with the earlier discussion about forgiveness.

9. Was Nietzsche right in advocating self-interest as the guiding principle of life, or was Jesus right in advocating self-giving love as the best path toward wholeness? Why?

10. Reflect on and discuss each phrase in the scriptural quotations about love (p. 45). What are the results when such wisdom is disregarded? How will your life change if scriptural wisdom is practiced more consistently?

11. What is the appropriate role of the community of believers in supporting each member's decision making?

12. How can members of a family best influence each other to develop a consistent personal value system?

Chapter Four

Freedom

Freedom is a profound human need, a characteristic of humanity at its best. From the earliest days of our lives, and as long as humans have walked the earth, people have desired to be free—free from constraint and from oppression, free to shape their lives by their decisions. Freedom is a necessary component of the process of growing to wholeness.

The majority of people who are alive today live in oppressive situations and suffer immense constraints on their freedom imposed by people who have power over them. For many, their decisions each day are primarily about survival. Often they are reduced to making inhuman choices: families live in hovels and do what they can to find their next meal; if they find work it is often poorly paid and dangerous to their health. Children are forced to work from an early age, as laborers or as soldiers or as victims of sexual degradation. Many lives, still in our time, are "nasty, brutish, and short." Such people experience almost no freedom, but they continue to yearn for freedom and they probably are aware that the powerful people of the world (including the middle class in Western society) are at least partly to blame for their condition.

Prosperous members of human society value their freedom and pass legislation to protect the rights they consider essential to preserve their freedom. Still, we in the wealthier societies often feel that our freedom is obstructed by illness or tragedy, by powerful structures like governments or corporations, by hurtful relationships, by the size of our mortgage or taxes or credit card debts, and even at times by our own selfishness. Rich or poor, young or old, robust or fragile, female or male, people everywhere feel a profound need for freedom.

Inner Freedom

This chapter has begun with a description of the situations in which all people, poor or rich, feel deprived of freedom, a vital component of wholeness. The purpose of the rest of the chapter is to turn our understanding of freedom toward our inner life: we are challenged to perceive ourselves as free humans, no matter what the circumstances. Inner freedom allows us to set the direction of our lives and grow toward wholeness in spite of the often overwhelming restrictions life imposes. That is the fundamental meaning of freedom in a religious sense.

In the Bible, God stands for freedom. The foundational Jewish experience of God was an experience of being set free. They had been an insignificant group of laborers, helpless and hopeless. God "redeemed" them from slavery, gave them a new sense of identity, and enabled them to embark on a community odyssey that continues to this day.

> "I will free you from the burdens of the Egyptians and deliver you from slavery to them. I will redeem you with an out-stretched arm . . ." (Exodus 6:6)

> "Do not fear, for I have redeemed you; I have called you by name, you are mine . . . For I am the LORD your God, the Holy One of Israel, your Savior." (Isaiah 43:1-3)

Notice that God, in these passages from the Hebrew Scriptures, is portrayed as both savior and redeemer, taking the initiative to set people free. There is no mention of a postbiblical Christian doctrine that God was delaying redemption or "holding a grudge" against humanity because of the sin of Adam and Eve.

The New Testament also teaches that Jesus came to set people free. "If the Son makes you free, you will be free indeed" (John 8:36). "You will know the truth, and the truth will make you free" (John 8:32). "For freedom Christ has set us free" (Galatians 5:1).

In Jesus' greatest concise description of his understanding of his own mission, he says, "The Son of Man came not to be served, but to be Servant, and to give his life to set people free" (Mark 10:45). (The verse is paraphrased; the last infinitive literally means to ransom or redeem.) That sentence deserves a whole chapter of reflective analysis, but it seems clear that Jesus understood his entire life's ministry as continuing the gracious initiative of God to save us, to redeem us, to set us free.

God continues to act in human life to set people free. It is not that God will be a sort of magical problem-solver and take away all the circumstances that distress us. Rather, God meets us at the depths of our being and helps us grow toward inner freedom, no matter what circumstances we endure. In this sense the South African hero Nelson Mandela was a free man in the depths of his heart through all his years in jail. We can be free people also, no matter what happens to us. With God's help we can overcome the constraints that bind us; we can set the course of our own lives; we can grow toward wholeness. Section 2 of this book discusses how we can understand God's action in our lives.

On a practical level most of us would benefit from considering the factors that restrict our freedom. These may include bad relationships, unhappy work environments, overwhelming debts, or oppressive authorities in society. Some people even oppress themselves from within by being too demanding (or not demanding enough) of themselves, or by constantly trying to please others.

The partners in every healthy relationship—friendship, partnership, and parent-child relationships—must respect and enhance each other's freedom. More will be found on this topic in the next chapter on emotional well-being, but some comments can also be offered in the current discussion of the importance of freedom for human wholeness.

Parenting for Freedom

The underlying purpose of parenting is to set young people free so that they can direct the course of their lives as mature and responsible humans. One of the most difficult issues for parents is striking a balance between discipline and freedom. The key is to enable children to make their own decisions as often as possible, as early as possible in their lives.

Younger children

Discipline means "setting limits with love." Parents have to set limits, but the key issue in limit-setting should be the safety of the child rather than the wishes of the parent. When parents need to modify the behavior of their children, love should always be part of the interaction. The love should be expressed, unconditionally if possible. To say "you're a bad boy (or girl)," or "you should be ashamed of yourself," is to attack the child personally. When parents say "you're a wonderful child and I love you, but you cannot keep doing that," the focus is on the child's *behavior*, not on the person. Consequences for misbehavior should be appropriate, immediate, and administered with respect. If a child considers a consequence unreasonable, listen to the child and negotiate.

Many parents are doubtless shaking their heads sadly or even scornfully at the foregoing opinions. While those ideas are admittedly idealistic, they will have a positive result if they are applied early enough in a child's life.

When parents bring unruly children to kindergarten and apprehensively wish the teacher "good luck," many teachers believe that the child's misbehavior is the product of parental shortcomings. Many children instinctively feel that their parents have no time for them, see them as a nuisance, impose commands without reasons, and do not listen to the children's concerns. Children who witness continual dissension between their parents or have suffered through the breakup of their parents' relationship are especially vulnerable. Often the children's reaction is to try to attract attention by misbehaving. Their misconduct should be corrected, but always on the basis of love, perhaps involving alterations in parents' behavior as well, especially in the realm of listening and taking more time to pay attention to the child.

Adolescents

Teenagers will always take risks, to the dismay of their parents. Such actions are part of their efforts to find their identity as independent individuals, setting the course of their own lives according to their own value systems. Such experimentation should be accepted as normal and inevitable. Young people will make mistakes, even serious ones, and may misuse their freedom and do harm to themselves and others. Parents' (and teachers') duty in those situations is to help the young person to face the consequences and learn from the mistakes. Serious irresponsibility and rebellion have to be confronted and discussed. Unfortunately, unsolvable issues in adolescent behavior can often be traced to problems in early childhood. The roots of misbehavior in a fifteen-year-old may be fifteen years (and possibly even several generations) deep.

Sometimes family relationships deteriorate to such an extent that conflict, disrespect, and resentment are the dominant characteristics of life at home. Only a major conversion by all parties can rescue the situation. In most cases it is up to the adults to take the initiative. Often even unexpected parental action and a sincere declaration of willingness to be more respectful, to listen, and to negotiate will be unable to penetrate the cloud of hostility. But such action may be worth trying, even as an option of last resort.

These opinions are obviously intended to challenge parents who believe their responsibility in the family is to give commands

and the children's duty is to obey. This chapter is an invitation
to negotiate with children about all kinds of issues that are traditionally considered appropriate matter for parental commands:
how much children are to eat, what children are to wear, how
much time they may spend on the telephone and computer, how
tidy they must keep their rooms, what they can and cannot do
"while you're living under my roof." There is no universal rule
about issues like these, but the proposal is that negotiation is
preferable to demanded obedience, from a very early age.

Obviously freedom must come to children by degrees, and the
dialogue between control and independence is a tension that begins early in a child's life and continues through the years of adolescence into adulthood. Many are the people who live in conflict
with their parents even well into adult life. Many are the adults
who continue to resist their parents' control even long after their
parents have died. They still refer to their parents in making difficult decisions, dealing with setbacks, and achieving success.

Young people recognize the need for limits on their behavior;
they want advice and support from their elders. But they also
want to be able to manage their own lives as much as possible—
who does not? We adults will help them best if we give them
opportunities for self-control and self-determination in their
lives as early and as often as possible. It is not easy, but the basic
orientation of our efforts must be to set our well-loved young
people free.

As long as life endures, the quest for freedom will be an indispensable component of the quest for wholeness.

Reflection Questions

1. What oppresses you—what factors keep you from feeling
   free—in your life at present?

2. For each element that restricts your freedom, decide whether
   the restriction is something you can accept and use as part

of your quest for wholeness, or whether the restriction must be fought against and eventually overcome.

3. For the restrictions that must be overcome, consider possible first steps. (Forthright discussion with someone else may be a vital beginning of the process.)

4. Discuss the principle that the ultimate goal of parenting is to set our children free.

5. Discuss the pros and cons of fostering children's freedom within limits that are primarily about safety and are always administered with perceptible love.

6. How can you give more freedom to the people with whom you are intimately involved? (Again, forthright discussion, especially with children, may be a useful first step.)

Chapter Five

Emotional Well-Being and Intimacy

Humans are body-beings capable of spiritual activity. Everything about our bodies is a fundamental part of who we are. All of us, whether male or female, need to reflect on and embrace our bodiliness as an indispensable component of our quest for wholeness. Some people are handsome or beautiful; others are considered plain. Some are strong; others are frail. Some are athletic; others are uncoordinated. The realm of sexuality is of paramount interest for some and worrisome for others. Some are highly expressive with regard to their feelings while others tend to be more reserved emotionally.

Every aspect of our bodily being is both an opportunity and a challenge in our personal journey. What other people think of us contributes to our self-awareness, but the foundation of wholeness is self-esteem based on true recognition of our abilities and shortcomings. Personal self-understanding and self-acceptance are essential components of everyone's journey toward wholeness.

You are invited to reflect on all of the several aspects of body-being that are mentioned in the first paragraph, but what follows in this chapter is a discussion about the value of emotional well-being and the qualities of valuable intimate relationships.

Many believers tend to regard emotions negatively. They have been taught that we are composed of body and soul, and that the soul is the noble and truly human part of our identity. The body and the emotions are often seen as diversions from what is truly important in life, enticing people to follow pathways that are unworthy of us as spiritual beings. Such attitudes arise from a commonly held understanding of humanity that is not based on Scripture, but rather has its roots in pre-Christian Greek philosophy. The distinction between these two understandings is so fundamental, and so unconsciously accepted, that it deserves several paragraphs of discussion.

Body and Soul: Philosophical Dualism

Most Christians have grown up with an understanding about humanity that originated in the philosophies of Plato and Aristotle: humans are a composite of body and soul. Aristotle's "rational animal" definition of humanity at least gave good emphasis to the bodily essence of our nature. (Later Christian philosophy preferred to refine the balance by describing humans as "incarnate spirits.") The idea that people are made of body and soul was adopted into European Christianity and became the predominant Christian viewpoint for centuries.

What few Christians realize is that, though Jesus lived a few centuries after the peak period of Greek philosophy, he did not understand humanity in the same way as Plato. Scriptural anthropology is fundamentally different from what most believers have been taught from childhood. Whether or not you prefer the Greek philosophical understanding about body and soul, we can surely agree that it is possible to believe in God and to be a faithful follower of Jesus without accepting the anthropology of Plato and Aristotle—because, as far as we know, Jesus himself was not familiar with their understanding of humanity, and he perceived human life as Jewish people always had. (See below for more details about the Jewish understanding.)

We can also believe in life beyond death without accepting the Greek view of humanity: in the New Testament, hope for life beyond death is not that the soul lives on in a heaven of souls ("immortality of the soul"), but that God will raise believers to new life so that they can participate in the ultimate reign of God ("resurrection"). Further discussion about life beyond death will be found in the last chapter of this book.

Greek philosophy understands human beings as composed of two opposed elements: a material body and a spiritual soul. The soul is seen as the life-principle in which reside all the more exalted human abilities: thinking, deciding, praying. The body, at best, is understood as a vehicle by which the soul can live in this world, learn through the senses, and communicate with others. At worst the body is seen as a trap, sometimes overwhelming the mind with emotion and deluding the soul by leading a person to pursue bodily attractions unworthy of a spiritual soul. At death only the body dies; the soul lives on in a spiritual world we have come to call "heaven," though in the Bible heaven is the home of God rather than the final destination of humans.

Such a dualistic philosophy can imply negative attitudes toward many aspects of human bodiliness—toward emotion, often toward women, and in particular toward sexuality. Especially in cultures originating in northern Europe, Christianity has suffered from such attitudes for centuries, and as a result some aspects of Christian tradition can be described as cold, legalistic, and intellectual.

Biblical "Unitary" Understanding: Body-Beings Capable of Spiritual Activity

It is a matter of surprise to many Christians that Jesus was the heir of a very different understanding about humanity. In the biblical tradition humans are not composed of two opposite elements (body and soul), but are "units." We are body-beings who can be soulful—who can think and love and create and hug and kiss and make decisions and know God and pray and dance and sing. Most people would call at least some of these activities "spiritual," even if we understand that they are done by body-beings.

In the scriptural understanding, the life-principle in a human being resides not in a soul that can live independently but in the creature's breath or in the blood. Thus, in the account in the book of Genesis, God breathed life into the first human. In the alternative image, "the life of the flesh is in the blood" (Leviticus 17:11). According to kosher rules, meat should have the blood drained out of it; humans should not eat the life of the animal because the life is God's gift. The blood of animals was used in rituals and sacrifices because the lifeblood offers a form of direct contact with God. That understanding of humanity also explains why Jesus gave us his *body and blood* in the Eucharist rather than his body and soul. For a Hebrew, "body and blood" means the whole living person.

This *unitary* way of describing humanity seems quite compatible with modern scientific understanding, which describes much of human activity in terms of brain complexity. Thinking, choosing, feeling emotion, sensing pain, and similar activities are described as the functions of our brains (rather than our souls). The difference between humans and animals is seen as a difference in brain complexity. Our brains are comparable to the brains of other creatures, but the decisive distinction seems to be that humans can perform functions other animals cannot. As far as we know, only humans can reflect on and evaluate their own behavior and find meaning in the events of their lives. What makes *homo sapiens* unique is self-consciousness. Many modern believers understand that ability as a matter of brain power: we do not need to imagine a soul directing our brain. Our brain directs our actions. When our brain's abilities are compromised, our human abilities are impeded. When our brain is dead, our life on earth is over.

For many contemporary people this unitary understanding of humanity is instinctively credible, and many are relieved to hear that it is compatible with the Bible, and with faith in God.

The biblical tradition is more positive about bodiliness, emotion, and sexuality than the European Christian adaptation of the Greek philosophical tradition. The ancient texts use bodily images about God, portraying God as planting a garden in Eden and shaping the body of the first human out of clay (Genesis 2:7-8), describing the heavens as "the work of [God's] fingers" (Psalm 8:3), presenting God as taking the people "up in my arms . . . like those who lift infants to their cheeks" (Hosea 11:3-4). God is presented as being emotionally very similar to humans, being pleased and being offended, rejoicing and regretting, being jealous and being compassionate. We even find images of God drawn from the realm of sexuality: "As the bridegroom rejoices over the bride, so shall your God rejoice over you" (Isaiah 62:5). "The children of the desolate woman will be more than the children of her that is married . . . for your Maker is your husband" (Isaiah 54:1, 5).

Scriptural writers did not need to explain that God does not really have fingers, arms, or sexuality. Writers and readers understood the deeper meaning of these poetic images and had no need to make theological statements about the spiritual nature of God. Their images express profound reality, and portray the goodness and God-likeness of human body-being.

Jesus, especially as he is presented in the Gospel of Mark, was a very emotional person. Confronted by a leper, Jesus is "moved with pity"—or possibly, according to some ancient manuscripts, he was moved with *anger* at the status to which society had reduced the suffering man (Mark 1:41). Preparing to cure a man's crippled hand in violation of traditional understanding of the Law of Moses, Jesus "looked around at them with anger; he was grieved at their hardness of heart" (Mark 3:5). Notice the emotion-words; do not let them slip past you because you have heard these accounts so often.

Responding to scribes' accusations that he is healing people by the power of Satan, Jesus is seething as he accuses his opponents of doing something that can never be forgiven—blaspheming against the Holy Spirit (Mark 3:28-29). When Jesus first forewarns his followers that he expects to be killed rather than to become the king-messiah they were anticipating, Peter protests, and Jesus, in a remarkable burst of emotion, accuses his friend of acting like Satan (Mark 8:33). The well-known scene of Jesus' driving out the merchants in the courtyard of the Temple (Mark 11:16-18) seems to be a carefully-calculated act of defiance against corrupt religious leadership rather than an emotional outburst. Admittedly, later evangelists excised most of Mark's portrayal of an emotional Jesus, but the evidence of this first-written gospel seems entirely believable and may give us all a sense of the importance of emotion in the search for wholeness.

Church Life

Emotional well-being is important also in the spiritual lives of believing adults. Ronald Rolheiser has written that our traditional proclamation of the Good News has made many people think they must choose either to be religious or to be emotional and sexual. He considers this a "tragic misunderstanding."[1] People have been taught that what they feel is often contrary to what is truly good. This is an unfortunate weakness in contemporary proclamation of the Gospel.

Churches ignore or belittle emotion at their peril. Instead, they should accomplish their goals by responding to the emotional needs of their adherents. The primary purpose of liturgy—the celebration of the sacraments, and the yearly schedule of festivals—is to support the faith of believers on an *emotional* level. The failure of contemporary liturgy to achieve that purpose is one of the fundamental reasons for the noninvolvement of a growing percentage of nominal members in all the "mainstream" Christian churches. People take part in liturgy in increasing numbers when their emotional needs are met—in evangelical communities, in churches where the music is appealing and modern, or even in parishes where the pastor is congenial rather than soulless. The celibacy required of the dedicated leaders in the

[1] Ronald Rolheiser, *The Holy Longing* (Cincinnati: St. Anthony Messenger Press, 2001), 6.

Roman Catholic Church is perceived by many members of the community as an obstacle to their credibility, and such members are becoming less compliant and less affiliated, generation after generation. One reason for the rapid growth experienced by evangelical and Pentecostal churches is their appeal to members' feelings of belonging, of rejoicing even in the midst of adversity, and of emotional involvement with each other and with God.

The Importance of Emotion and Intimacy in the Lifelong Quest for Wholeness

Personal growth is built on a series of intimate relationships, from parent-child intimacy to childhood friendships to more mature and more intimate friendships to faithful, lifelong commitment.

Everyone's first intimate experience was the hugs and kisses we received minutes after we were born. The emotional love of parents for their children is an indispensable starting point for the children's quest for wholeness. Children who are forced by circumstance to survive in a love-deprived environment have immense obstacles to overcome. Children who grow up in an atmosphere of being loved and expressing love for others are well launched on the quest.

It is important for people of every age to feel affirmed in their emotional lives. If we feel delight in a given situation we should believe that our emotions are telling us the truth, and enjoy the pleasure. If we feel angry, we probably have a good reason for that feeling. Of course, there are valid ways and harmful ways of expressing our feelings, but the underlying attitude of observers toward expressions of emotion should be affirmation. Instead of attempting to end a debate by saying "don't get emotional about this issue," we should be listening intently to what the emotional person is trying to express. Instead of demanding that children stop crying we should encourage them to tell us about what is upsetting them, listen positively to what they are saying, and help them work toward a solution. Instead of demanding that children end friendships we perceive to be problematic, we should discuss their perceptions of the values and drawbacks of the friendship and help them decide for themselves. Idealistic proposals like those in the last few sentences, admittedly, depend on lifelong feelings of love and trust between parent and child.

Of course, uncontrolled expression of emotion is not part of well-being at any stage of human growth. Emotion must be balanced by mind, will, religious wisdom, and community standards. Still, the reciprocal is also true: *emotion* should influence *mind*, will, and religious wisdom as people seek a healthy balance in their lives. People who act in the name of responsible emotion against racial, economic, or religious strictures may well be growing toward wholeness, regardless of the consequences they may suffer as a result. People who are emotionally inspired to participate in reform movements may be right, though traditions and the leaders of the community may proclaim that they are wrong or even evil.

The intimacy of friendship is an important part of emotional well-being, beginning early in life, continuing through the years of childhood and adolescence, and never ceasing to be important, even in the lives of retired people. Friendship is vitally important to children's well-being, and good friendships should be encouraged and supported. "Peer pressure" by good friends is often a positive influence in people's lives: friends help each other to deal with life's hardships; friends encourage each other to keep trying; friends smarten each other up when somebody does something foolish. Friends are our best support in life's quest for wholeness.

"Young love" is beautiful and all-involving; it should be affirmed and never scorned. Young people give and receive affirmation, loyalty, generosity, and great happiness in relationships of progressive intimacy. They also get hurt at times, but the experience of desolation, too, can be an opportunity for growth. It is not valuable for young people to be told they should not engage in loving friendships at their age on the grounds that they will experience great regret when the relationships end.

Almost everyone is going to be "dumped" sooner or later; tearful expressions of the resulting feelings are valid and normal. Young people may need to be helped (by friends or possibly by parents or teachers) to learn from such experiences and to go forward wiser and more confident.

A sexual component is to be expected in adolescent and adult relationships. Sexuality includes the entire range of feelings and behaviors by which human beings express themselves through look, touch, word, and action. As people grow through adolescence, their sexuality becomes more overt in their personalities and in their relationships. Young people's sexual expression will naturally take many forms, involving more or less complete activity. Like all intimate relationships, those with a sexual component can be tremendously beneficial or tremendously hurtful.

Key Components of Successful Relationships: Honesty, Equality, Responsibility

All relationships are complex, but it may be possible to use relatively simple terms to describe what is needed for success— whether we are describing childhood friendships, progressively more intimate relationships among young people, relationships that may become lifelong and loving, or friendships among adults, young or older. All such relationships are primarily emotional and should be affirmed as such. All of them are essential to each human's quest for wholeness.

We have already discussed the importance of a sense of direction in life, a consistent personal value system, and the kind of freedom that allows us to set the course of our lives, with due regard for the circumstances. All these elements of wholeness are an important foundation for emotional well-being and successful relationships.

What characteristics can be found in every good relationship? To put it simply, all of us should do our best to make our relationships honest, equal, and responsible. Put more negatively, we must help each other, and we must enhance our own growth by removing three deadly factors from all intimate relationships: deception, oppression, and irresponsibility.

Honesty

It seems self-evident that we should be sincere in expressing ourselves to those we love. We are not called to be brutal in our honesty; there is room for consideration of the other person's feelings. Always there should be a place for respectful disagreement. But self-interested dishonesty in speech or action is always destructive. Sadly, too many people are habitually dishonest with their closest friends and loved ones.

Perhaps the most common example is speaking ill "behind a friend's back." Instead of engaging in constructive discussion, people often express their complaints in the absence of a friend, and cause others to think badly of or even to ostracize the victim. It is a practice that seems to begin rather early in childhood, is unfortunately characteristic of the school years, and continues even among adults who consider themselves highly principled.

Dishonesty about sexuality and intimate relationships is another common destructive practice. Even young students can make a long list of the lies people tell each other to achieve sexual intimacy. A very damaging lie is "I love you," when it is spoken for selfish purposes by people who feel no such commitment. There are lies about one's intentions as intimate moments begin, lies about past activity, and lies about dangers and precautions.

The worst dishonesty in a committed relationship is sexual unfaithfulness. It is the only sexual offense listed in the Ten Commandments, and the only one Jesus spoke against. In this, our long-standing tradition is wise and true. Most people in committed relationships expect their partners to be faithful. Adultery is harmful to a relationship whether it is discovered or not; when it becomes known, it destroys the victim's self-esteem and security and is devastating to the trust on which the relationship is based.

When partners embark on a friendship or a committed relationship, they are amalgamating their individual quests for wholeness. They decide that they can best be true to themselves by living in a loving relationship with another. They are forever part of each other's life journey, each other's story of salvation. When they experience dishonesty by a friend or partner their quest is seriously compromised. Major healing is required before there can be renewal of purpose, either within or beyond the relationship.

Honesty is an essential component of relationships. Always be trustworthy. Never lie about love; never lie to someone you care about; never injure a friend by speaking evil without the friend's knowledge. And never allow yourself to be lied to. Be trustful, but be aware. Recognize the "familiar lies" when you hear them; be confident in your own worth. Build relationships that will be long-lasting and beneficial, both to you and to the people you love.

Equality

No relationship can be perfectly equal. Some people tend to take the lead and others prefer to follow. Some are persuasive and others are accepting. Healthy relationships are always based on respect and concern for the other person's welfare. Any example of oppression in a relationship is always harmful.

The relationship between parents and their children is not a relationship between equal partners, but it should be characterized by mutual respect and consideration and not by oppressive behavior. When asked: "why do you think parents decide to have children?" ten-year-old students have been heard to reply: "so they can have someone to order around and make them do jobs." On the other hand, regrettably often, children of all ages are described as disrespectful toward their parents, and family life is harsh and often nasty as a result.

This paragraph is intended to invite parents (and prospective parents) never to allow their behavior toward their children to be oppressive in any way. Having little time to play with children, repeatedly refusing children's requests, setting limits that have nothing to do with safety and are really based on parents' wishes, demanding obedience to arbitrary commands, and imposing excessive consequences for misbehavior—any of these "typical" parental practices may give rise to children's instinctive feelings of being oppressed. It is not surprising when the children respond in kind, and disrespect becomes the trademark of the relationship.

In contemporary educational circles a growing number of students consistently oppress others. Bullies cause physical harm, but also damage the spirits of their victims. Circles of friends often become jungles of dissension, with tyrannical or "bossy" leaders and unpredictable patterns of exclusion and submission. Serious problems of depression and inertia are often the results.

Everyone accepts in theory that mutual respect and concern for the other person's well-being is of great importance for healthy relationships. It may seem inappropriate to spend so long speaking of oppressive behavior in paragraphs devoted to promoting equality in relationships, but many people do not perceive that their own behavior may be unintentionally oppressive. The foregoing examples are offered as an opportunity for self-evaluation.

As relationships become more intimate, young people put all kinds of pressure on each other. The theme of conquest is played out in hundreds of variations in intimate relationships, and all of them are destructive. Every thoughtful person would surely agree that it is always wrong to continue sexual activity aggressively after the other person says "stop," to make fun of another person's hesitation, to boast about "scores," to terrify a companion by driving recklessly, to take someone to a lonely place against the person's wishes, to hang on to a person's arm to keep the person from leaving the room. Those are all examples of oppressive behavior; there are hundreds more.

Oppression often continues in partnerships that are intended to be long-lasting and loving. It may be that partners' attempts to exert power are based in the selfish expectation that their wishes will be met, with little consideration for the needs and hopes of the beloved. Newspapers often report the tragic results when men who have been brought up in a culture of male dominance (Christian or Muslim; of European, African, or Asian heritage) react violently to women who decide not to submit to further humiliation. Spouses of either sex who bully their partners are doomed to produce an unhappy home.

Oppressive behavior must be recognized and named for what it is. If a partner expresses the feeling that a certain behavior is unwelcome, the feeling must be respected and responded to. There are rules for "fair fighting" or conflict resolution that may help people solve disagreements in an atmosphere of respect. Professional counselors may be helpful in some situations.

People who are at peace within themselves are much less likely to resort to oppressive behavior in relationships. Mutual respect and self-giving concern for the other are necessary elements of healthy friendships and intimate relationships, and such relationships are an integral part of every human's quest for wholeness.

Responsibility

To describe healthy intimate relationships as "responsible" is to say that the partners must consider factors beyond their own personal wishes. In everything we do, we are part of a number of communities. No one grows to wholeness in isolation. All of us have responsibilities to those with whom we are intimate, and also to our families of origin, our heritage, our neighbors, our friends and colleagues, our churches, our political communities, and indeed to the entire family of humanity and to the planet Earth.

It is not that every intimate action has to be conscious of all those areas of responsibility, but it remains valuable to realize that we all live in a context, a network of people who are affected by the decisions each of us makes in our personal quest for wholeness. It is not that we can never decide to act against tradition, or against the wishes of our family, or in a way that will not be approved by the wider community. But when we do make such choices, we should act responsibly: we should be aware of the implications of our actions and their effect on others.

Parents who are continually angry with each other and their children should consider the effect their dissension is having, especially on their children, and should reconsider their priorities and modify their behavior with regard to these most intimate of relationships.

Children who bully others must consider what kind of persons they are making of themselves and realize the harm they are doing to their victims and to their circle of friends and classmates. Parents of such bullies should consider their responsibility in perhaps having contributed to such behavior, and their duty to take responsible steps to alleviate it.

The issue of intimate relationships among unmarried people under the age of thirty is difficult to discuss. We have no wisdom from Jesus about these issues. In his day people married when they reached the age of puberty. The values we consider traditional have been developed in society (including pre-Christian society) over many centuries.

A revised set of values is now being developed by the current generations in the course of their lived emotional experience. Most young people would agree that relationships should be honest, that oppression is wrong in intimate situations, and that it is important to be responsible, particularly in sexual activity. Those three considerations form the basis of the revising of contemporary values with regard to intimacy.

Many older people take issue with developments in contemporary social behavior, primarily out of concern for the associated dangers. The battle of statistics rages on: 50 percent of students have engaged in sexual intercourse by the age of sixteen; 70 percent of people live together before entering marriage; sexually-transmitted infections (STIs) are increasing; a shocking number of North American couples are childless and infertile, often as a consequence of STIs; teenage pregnancy is not increasing exponentially but is always a cause of life-altering distress and results in abortion in a regrettable number of cases; divorce is increasing and is more frequent among couples who lived together before marrying. People may modify their behavior to some extent in response to such statistics, but the evolution of values will continue, and it already involves a large majority of people between the ages of fourteen and thirty.

Adult attitudes regarding female and male young people are particularly delicate. Almost every parent of girls believes that they must be treated differently from boys and that their behavior must be more rigidly controlled, especially with regard to relationships. It is certainly true in practice that unwise behavior by girls and young women involves much more serious consequences than unwise behavior by boys. As a parent of three sons, I realize that my opinions will be disparaged, but I will speak them nonetheless. Responsible behavior is characteristic of girls and young women, and their ability to make wise decisions should be respected. They deserve honest and forthright discussion about the values and dangers of intimate relationships and establishing safeguards for recognizing and responding to potentially threatening or uncomfortable situations. Even with teenagers, attempting to control the behavior of young females is not beneficial; it will only inspire resentment and clever methods to avoid scrutiny. The most useful strategy is respectful discussion, with a clear statement of the elders' values and the reasons for them, and clear recognition that the decisions are not the responsibility of the elders but of the young people.

Those who are deeply concerned about these developments must devise improved strategies to promote values they hold dear. Perhaps the best we can do is to help each other form healthy intimate relationships and support each other when the foreseeable adversity strikes. Young people are willing to listen to traditional wisdom presented strongly and credibly; they are not receptive to "preaching," demands, ultimatums, or attempts at control by their elders. They want to be encouraged as they form intimate relationships; they need to be helped to recognize the destructive elements that can enter relationships; they value wisdom about how to develop healthy relationships; they need to consider how to be responsible. Most of them hope for the loving, faithful, lifelong commitment that characterizes the best sexual relationships. They want to be reminded of traditional values. And they want to decide for themselves.

Conclusion

Emotional well-being and intimacy are important components of everyone's quest for wholeness. Following the example of the community that gave us the Scriptures as a guide for our journey, believing communities should be more accepting of human bodiliness, of emotionality, and of sexuality. Believers should find ways to help each other identify and achieve what is needed for emotional well-being and healthy intimate relationships.

Reflection Questions

1. Discuss the advantages and disadvantages of understanding humans as body-beings capable of spiritual activity, rather than as composites of body and soul.

2. To what extent do you agree that our emotions usually tell us the truth?

3. Give examples from intimate relationships of the good effects of honesty, equality, and responsibility, and the ill effects of dishonesty, oppression, and irresponsibility.

4. What other characteristics of healthy intimate relationships would you add?

5. Describe what you consider to be a credible value system for the future with regard to sexual relationships.

PART TWO

Finding God in Contemporary Life

In this second section of *What Makes Us Whole* we will search for credible ways of speaking about the role of God in our lives. This search is not new; it has been going on for thousands of years in the Jewish and Christian traditions. The scriptural accounts of God's interventions in human history have given rise to a centuries-long search for a more complete understanding of God. Theologians of all religious traditions seek to formulate credible statements about God. More than 800 years ago St. Thomas Aquinas stated that everything we say about God is more false than it is true, since the reality of God is so far beyond our ability to understand. Near the end of his life he declared that everything he had written was worth no more than a pile of straw. Still, his ideas have been preserved and reflected upon for many centuries, and people of every age have struggled with the same quandary. Fully admitting that our efforts will be worth even less than straw, we will attempt to discuss these difficult fundamental questions: Who is God? How does God affect our lives?

Both the Bible and classic European art use images that compare God to various aspects of human life. We have few ways

73

to imagine God that are not based on human imagery. While realizing that the reality of God is vastly different from that of humanity, and that God is a spiritual reality, many adults have still not replaced childish anthropomorphic (human-like) images of God. As adults we need to search for understandings of God that, while never able to explain the reality, will at least attempt to respond to questions that have developed in our minds since we stopped attending Sunday school or taking theology courses. The search for better knowledge of the unknowable is the exploration of mystery.

"Mystery" is an important concept in religious discussions. Too often the word is used to end a theological discussion: "It's a mystery; you either believe it or you don't." To use "mystery" for that purpose is a poor excuse for shortage of ideas.

Mystery is something you can learn more and more about without completely exhausting the topic. Every human being is a mystery in that sense. The people we live with and love are good examples of mysteries: we can learn more and more about them at deep personal levels and yet never say we understand them completely. Our spouse or partner, and particularly our children, repeatedly say or do the unexpected, and open new vistas in our understanding of them.

In religious thought, God is the ultimate mystery, the never-ending surprise. What we say about God, guided by the revelation and insight of the Scriptures and our faith tradition, can express truth about God, but all such expressions are partial and often leave questions that require further discussion. Understandings that satisfied believers in centuries past may no longer be adequate for contemporary believers. Some traditional ways of speaking about God can, on reflection, be said to be so unsatisfactory that they must be abandoned. Always we try to ask new questions, make new comparisons, search for new insight. We know we will never understand God completely, but it is essential to our human identity to keep trying, and to keep learning more.

In this section we intend honestly to confront ideas about God that are no longer satisfactory, and to look for the most believable ways of speaking of God for people of our time. We will point out the inadequacy of physical images of God found in many works of art. We will reject images of God as a warrior, including such familiar language as "the Lord of Hosts." We will express ambivalence about speaking of God as a father or as a mother: they are both beautiful images, and yet they both have limitations. Most difficult of the concepts that must be explored critically is the idea that God causes everything that happens in our world. It is a widely-believed item of faith, but it is extremely problematic for a great many people who want to believe, but who are not satisfied by traditional understandings. We will attempt to express the attributes of God in a positive way that emphasizes that the power of God is spiritual. Most fundamental will be a discussion about what is meant when the New Testament says "God is love."

In this section of the book we will alternate between discussions of inadequate ideas of God and suggestions about more believable understandings. We will assert that God is a spiritual reality, powerful and transforming in the ways that love is powerful and transforming. It is hoped that by the end of this section a valuable constellation of credible ideas will have emerged.

Chapter Six

Physical Images of God

The Bible presents God by using *literary* images of emotion and power based in human experience. As mentioned in the chapter on emotional well-being, writers and readers understood the deeper meaning of these poetic images and had no need to make theological statements about the spiritual nature of God. Their images expressed profound reality. Through the Christian centuries God has been portrayed by means of a variety of *artistic* images. Christian pictorial art has portrayed God in ways that may express a modicum of truth, if properly understood, but are also dreadfully inadequate and may lead to misunderstandings that endanger the development of mature faith.

In one of the most familiar and unfortunate of traditional images God is portrayed as an old man. Some descriptions found in the Bible have been immortalized in Christian art—with the result that for many Christians of European heritage God is an old *white* man, sometimes visualized as sitting on a throne somewhere in a heaven in the sky. Michelangelo's "Creation of Adam" at the center of the Sistine Chapel ceiling is a prime example of imagery we have considered acceptable, though it is both gender-biased and culturally limited in portraying God as an aging male human of European coloring.

Teachers and parents have long been convinced that children's minds cannot understand the realm of the spiritual on their own. They are thought to need "concrete" physical, tangible images to help them understand the immaterial, mystical sphere. In the same vein, church leaders in the past felt that uneducated peasant believers needed tangible images to support their faith. The sacraments helped to provide some of the needed images, but their symbolic value was often misinterpreted because of an overuse of physical terminology (so, for example, children tried to peer into chalices to see the blood of Jesus). Art became the chosen vehicle for expressing the spiritual reality of God.

Many people realize that artistic portrayals are symbolic, but we subconsciously retain the first images we received and pass them on to our children. Some believers say they are quite satisfied with images of "God in the sky" and that they want to pass on these images to their children. One parent forcefully argued: "I want my children to believe in Santa Claus; it's a beautiful custom. And I want my child to believe that God is sitting up in heaven watching over us." Recognizing the merit of that sentiment, I still feel we must deal with the question about "what do we tell our children when they realize that Santa has been living with them all year long?" And when, and how, do we help our children deal with the realization that their belief in "God in the sky" is inadequate to sustain their faith as adults? Far too many adults in our society think that religion, like Santa Claus, is for children; as adults they no longer believe what they were taught about faith as children, and they have never developed an adult understanding about God and faith.

As intelligent believers, we must make a conscious effort to realize the damage that is done by taking biblical and artistic imagery literally, and we must search for ways to understand the reality of God in a credible way. Perhaps we can develop more satisfactory images to teach to our children so that, as they become more mature, they will not be forced to "unlearn" all they have been taught as children. Attempts to develop credible images about the spiritual nature of God, even for children, will be made in later chapters.

The Second Commandment

Remarkably, the Jewish tradition has known from the outset the danger of portraying God through physical images. The second commandment, which has literally been deleted from the Christian list of the Ten Commandments, has always been understood in the Jewish tradition to forbid any kind of representational art about God—or anything else, for that matter.

> You shall not make for yourself an idol, whether in the form of anything that is in heaven above, or that is on the earth beneath, or that is in the water under the earth. (Exodus 20:4)

Christian tradition has understood this commandment to mean the same as the first commandment, requiring that believers have no other god than the one God, and forbidding worship of idols. As a result, we have omitted the second commandment as it is quoted above from our list of the ten. (The traditional number of commandments was retained by dividing the tenth commandment into two parts.) Jews and Muslims understand the word translated as "idol" to mean *any* "carved image." As a result, they have always retained this verse as a distinct second commandment. They understand it to mean that no work of art should ever attempt to portray God, because God is far beyond human imagining or understanding. The same religious traditions further prohibit representational art of any kind because of the fear that images can become idols and people will pray to the statue instead of to the one it attempts to represent.

That is why there has been almost no Jewish or Muslim representational religious art. Judaism and Islam are religions based on literature (the Scriptures), not on pictorial art. Repeated warfare and frequent migrations may explain the almost total absence of Jewish art from the biblical era, but the strict traditional interpretation of the second commandment is probably the main reason that so little art has been found. Jewish representational art on religious topics began to appear only in the twentieth century CE, when Marc Chagall, a Russian-born French Jewish artist, broke the tradition of centuries and portrayed episodes from the Bible. To this day most synagogues and mosques are decorated by very elaborate patterns, but they have no representational art, and they absolutely never attempt to show God, least of all as an old man sitting on a throne.

The purpose of this chapter is to propose that the Jewish tradition was very wise in prohibiting artistic representations of God, or of anything that might be converted into an idol. Idolatry was an explicit danger in their society; many men found pagan religions more attractive than the religion of Moses, partly because of associated ecstatic and orgiastic observances. Idolatry in our day is more implicit: many contemporary people worship the almighty dollar and do not realize that it has replaced faith as the central focus of their lives.

The prophet Isaiah satirized pagan sculptors who carved statues from a block of wood and then worshiped them:

> [The carpenter] cuts down cedars or chooses a holm tree or an oak . . . . Part of it he takes and warms himself; he kindles a fire and bakes bread. . . . The rest of it he makes into a god, his idol, bows down to it and worships it . . . . [These idols] do not know, nor do they comprehend; for their eyes are shut, so that they cannot see, and their minds as well, so that they cannot understand. . . . a deluded mind has led him astray, and he cannot . . . say, "Is not this thing in my right hand a fraud?" (Isaiah 44:14-20)

> The idols of the nations are silver and gold,
>   the work of human hands.
> They have mouths, but they do not speak;
>   they have eyes, but they do not see . . .
> Those who make them
>   and all who trust them
>   shall become like them. (Psalm 135:15-18)

The Jewish tradition knew that people might idolize any artistic representation of "anything that is in heaven above, or that is on the earth beneath, or that is in the water under the earth" (Exodus 20:4). From the earliest Christian times the church has chosen to ignore the wisdom of the second commandment. There have been movements within Christianity over the centuries that have recognized the value of the second commandment and have accepted the truth that to express the greatness of God is far beyond the ability of concrete images. Some such movements even sought to destroy all the religious symbols they could find in homes, churches, and galleries. Others, less violent, have simply created places of worship that are free of representational artistic images, in a spirit of faithfulness to God's commandment as it is also interpreted in Jewish and Muslim places of worship.

In a way, we of the "graphic-friendly traditions" have created idolatrous images of our own—not that we worship statues, but that our practices are based on erroneous ideas, such as that God can be accurately portrayed by images of white-skinned men.

This discussion is not intended to disagree with artistic portrayals of *Jesus*, who was, of course, a male human who lived among us. It is still important to realize, though, that Jesus was a person of Palestine, not of Europe. He was not tall, with blue eyes and chestnut hair, as so many European artists and film directors have portrayed him. He was likely short, with dark eyes, black hair, and dark skin, and possibly stocky and muscular because of his lifelong work in the construction industry. Again, our traditional art has betrayed us and led to discriminatory attitudes.

Whatever you think of this discussion, it is important to be well aware of the shortcomings of concrete images of God the Creator, and not to teach our children ideas about God that they will have to unlearn (often without adequate support systems) as they mature. The attempt to find credible ways of speaking about God, even to children, is the purpose of this section of *What Makes Us Whole*.

Reflection Questions

1. List and consider the advantages and disadvantages of artistic images of God, both for children and for adults.

2. What is your opinion of the value of classical European religious art? of Christian religious art from Africa and Asia?

3. Why do you think we should (or should not) continue to disregard the literal meaning of the second commandment?

Chapter Seven

"In the Image of God"

So God created humankind in his image,
in the image of God he created them;
male and female he created them.

(Genesis 1:27)

Many children have come to believe that this passage demonstrates that God looks like a human, and indeed a human of the male gender. Usually the passage is translated using masculine English pronouns, but in the original Hebrew text (as in Italian and many other languages) there is no pronoun expressed: the verb "created" implies a pronoun, which could be "he," "she," or "it" in English. That is why I would prefer to use the gender-inclusive word "God" rather than the pronouns "his" and "he" in presenting that verse, however repetitive and awkward it would seem.

To say that we are created in God's image does *not* mean that God looks like a human, or that humans look like God, or that God is male. The Roman Catholic bishops of Canada, in a discussion about the "image of God" in humanity, have stated that "God is neither male nor female, nor a combination of male and female."[1] So in what way are humans created in the image of God?

The image of God in humanity is found not in the way we look, but in what we can do. We are "image of God" when we love, when we think, when we decide, when we create (in all the meanings of creativity). In another way, we can realize that we are image of God when we dance and hug and work and play—because all the best human actions, including bodily actions, show forth the greatness and complexity of the spiritual God.

In a further explanation that may be dismissed as overly academic, some scholars point out a parallelism in Genesis 1:27 that is very typical of Hebrew poetry.

In the image of God	*he created them;*
Male and female	*he created them.*

Those two lines clearly have a parallel structure. Parallel lines mean the same thing, expressed in different words. In verse 27, "in the image of God" and "male and female" are parallel elements. Some commentators believe that the author intended the parallelism to convey that maleness and femaleness, the sexual nature of humanity, is a profound image of God. The way men and women complement each other, are incomplete without each other, can be part of each other, can love each other, can create together—what men and women can *do*—is the best "image of God" in humanity. It is not within the intention of that interpretation to demean the lives of people who are celibate or unmarried or homosexual. Rather, the interpretation expresses in the abstract that the fact that humanity is gendered and sexual is one of the best images to help us understand what God is like.

Just as maleness and femaleness are complementary aspects of humanity, so humanity is incomplete without God. The self-giving

---

[1] *Roots: Finding Strength in Biblical Tradition* (Ottawa, ON: The Canadian Conference of Catholic Bishops, 1991), chap. 10, "Just Who Are You, God?"

love of humans is an image of the loving-kindness of God. Human love can help us realize that God's love is transforming, healing, and creative. As mentioned earlier in this book, the Bible sometimes uses sexual images to describe God's relationship with people.

At the same time, the Bible realized that people often misuse sexuality and do great harm to each other. Like all images, human activity is an ambivalent image of the greatness of God. We understand what God is like by observing the good things people do. Sometimes, in the past, even evil things that people do were interpreted as images of what God is like. Thus God has been portrayed as a vicious warrior in the Scriptures because in biblical times war was considered essential to survival, and victory in war was God's gift. God has also been portrayed as a vengeful patriarchal power because at that time male dominance was considered good and essential (at least by male authors).

We must constantly purify our images and understanding of God, but the principle remains valid: The image of God in humanity is found in the good things humans can do.

Reflection Questions

1. Give specific anecdotes that illustrate the truth that human actions can be an image of God. Recall and tell stories in which people have done things that helped you realize what God is like.

2. Comment on the interpretation that one of the best images of God in humanity is our sexuality. Part of the discussion may involve the realization that sexuality, like all human comparisons about God, often provides a flawed image.

Chapter Eight

The Lord of Hosts

One biblical image of God that is often used unconsciously or without adequate reflection is that of God as a warrior.

A "lord" is defined in dictionaries as "the male head of a household,"[1] "a man of rank or high position,"[2] and "a man who has considerable power, authority or influence over others."[3] A "host" is "an army, a multitude, a great number,"[4] "a very large number of people or things, an army (archaic)."[5]

"Lord of Hosts" refers to God as the military leader of the people of Israel. Most believers would protest that they don't think of God in that sense, even when they say those words. But we should be aware that such is the literal meaning of these

---

[1] Merriam-Webster's Collegiate Dictionary (11th ed., 2004) offers this as its third definition of "lord," but calls "male head of household" obsolete.

[2] Merriam-Webster online Dictionary http://www.merriam-webster.com/dictionary/lord.

[3] Encarta World English Dictionary embedded in Microsoft Word 2004 for Macintosh (version 11.3.5)

[4] In http://www.yourdictionary.com/host.

[5] Encarta World English Dictionary embedded in MSWord 2004 for Macintosh (version 11.3.5). The idea that these usages are described as archaic or obsolete (and also are gender-exclusive) is part of the reason that these terms should be deleted from Christian language about God.

images that have become so familiar to us. For many centuries, the God of Moses was understood as a god of military might.

One of God's basic promises in the book of Exodus was to give the Jewish people a land of their own—a land God would take from "the Canaanites, the Hittites, the Amorites, the Perizzites, the Hivites, and the Jebusites" (Exodus 3:8). According to a foundational tenet of Jewish tradition, then, God was going to take the territory away from the people who were living in it and give it as "the promised land" to "the chosen people." I have heard many people of Palestine (a word that literally means "land of the Philistines") decry the idea that God, repeatedly through the centuries, has decided to take their homeland away from them and give it to the "chosen people." Consider how it feels to read the ancient stories if your heritage is Egyptian or Syro-Phoenician (Lebanese) or Ammonite. (Amman is the capital city of the contemporary kingdom of Jordan.)

The idea that the Promised Land is God's gift to the Jewish people continues to be at the root of conflict in the Holy Land to this day. It should not be part of a lasting credible theology for believers—but in fact it is, very much so. Evangelical Christians, who have achieved significant political power in the United States, are convinced that God will take the Land away from its Palestinian inhabitants and restore it to the Jewish people before the eagerly-anticipated final coming of the kingdom of God. According to some observers it is not primarily Jewish voters, but rather evangelical voters, who inspire the United States' huge investment in the defense of the state of Israel.

In the book of Exodus, God is portrayed as defeating the Egyptian army by drowning them, prompting the triumphant canticle of Exodus 15:

> The LORD is a warrior;
> the LORD is his name. . . .
> Your right hand, O LORD,
> . . . shattered the enemy . . .
> . . . you sent out your fury; it consumed them like stubble.
> (Exodus 15:3, 6, 7)

Another "academic" distinction is necessary: "The LORD is his name" is not a correct translation of the Hebrew text. In fact, every time you see LORD spelled in capital letters in the Hebrew Scriptures, what actually appears in the text is not the word "lord," but the sacred name of God that was given to Moses in Exodus 3:13-16.

Because of a strict traditional interpretation of the third commandment, which we learned as "You are not to take the name of the LORD your God in vain," the sacred name of God is never pronounced by Jewish believers, not even when it appears in the Scriptures being read in the synagogue. You also may have seen the word spelled "G_d" in documents by Jewish writers: such is their respect for the name of God that they not only will not pronounce the Name but they respectfully do not even spell out the word "God." We Christians, who feel free to pronounce the Hebrew name of God despite Jewish protests, and who often thoughtlessly use the name of God and Jesus without reverence, can surely learn about respect for God from these faithful Jewish people.

Most likely you have heard the sacred Name of God pronounced or sung in Christian circles, but we will not reproduce it here out of respect for Jewish tradition. (The first syllable of God's name in Hebrew is the last syllable of words like hallelujah, Isaiah, and Jeremiah.)

Rather than pronounce the sacred Name, Jewish tradition chose to replace it, whenever it appears in the Bible, with the Hebrew word *ʾadonai*, meaning "my lord." In modern translations, it is written in capital letters (LORD) to advise the reader that what is really in the text is not *ʾadonai* but rather the never-spoken sacred Name of God.

It is not appropriate for a Christian to comment on this Jewish tradition, but a remark about Christian practice may be of interest. Christians have uncritically accepted the Jewish usage, with the result that we constantly speak of God as "the Lord." Many of us now cringe at the phrase, because when we refer to God as "the Lord" or "the Lord of hosts," we are perpetuating the image of God as a dominant male and a fearsome warrior.

To continue a brief summary of military images of God in the Bible, the books of Joshua and Judges narrate the conquest of Palestine by Jewish armies under the guidance and protection of a bloodthirsty God who orders and supports massacre and torture. Later, in the course of David's rise to power, his predecessor Saul offers the hand of his daughter Michal in marriage and asks for one hundred Philistine foreskins as a "marriage present." (Do you imagine that the foreskins were surgically removed?) David's success in providing the required marriage gift makes Saul realize that "the LORD was with David" (1 Samuel 18:20-28).

This militaristic portrayal of God continued for centuries. Many psalms call upon God to "break the teeth of the wicked" (Psalm 3:7), "rise up . . . in your anger" (Psalm 7:6), "answer . . . from his holy heaven with mighty victories by his right hand" (Psalm 20:6), "take hold of shield and buckler . . . draw the spear and javelin against my pursuers" (Psalm 35:2). Perhaps the most horrifying line in the entire Bible is found in an otherwise-beautiful and well-known psalm of lament, written after the destruction of Jerusalem, speaking resentfully about the Babylonian conquerors: "Happy shall they be who take your little ones and dash them against the rock!" (Psalm 137:9).

Of course there are many wonderful and believable images of God to be found in the Scriptures. We will get to them later. Not only Christians, but also many Jewish religious thinkers reject these militaristic ideas about God. Some mainstream Christian churches have taken steps to reduce references to war in hymns and readings, with the resultant loss of standards like "Onward Christian Soldiers" and "A Mighty Fortress Is Our God." Many Jewish leaders express similar concern. Instead of "Lord" as a substitute for the sacred Name of God, some of them use the Hebrew word *hashem* ("the Name") wherever the sacred Name appears.

We have dealt with this topic at some length for a number of purposes: all believers must come to terms with the realization that we need to be selective: we must endorse images of God in our tradition that foster mature faith, and reject images of God that are no longer acceptable. It is entirely justifiable to say: "We don't think about God as a warrior any more, even though these images are found in the Scriptures." But the images endure in our subconscious as a result of repetition. Warrior images must be gradually trimmed from our lexicon about God.

One of the best ways to reduce that subliminal sense of God as a warrior is to reduce the use of the terms "Lord" and "Lord of Hosts" in our prayers. The term "Lord" is everywhere. It is of questionable value since it portrays God, in the most benign understanding, by using the image of a dominant male. (There are no female lords.) It is true that we are called to accept God's greatness and to allow God to rule our lives. Still, surely we do not always have to use an image that was born out of people's desire for military victory. Instead of constantly and mindlessly calling God "the Lord," could we not address God just as "our God," or as our Creator, our Savior, our Redeemer, God of love, gracious God . . . ? Instead of "Let us pray to the Lord: Lord, hear our prayer," we could use a variety of invocations, for example, "Let us pray together: Gracious God, hear us."

Thus far this section called "Finding God in Contemporary Life" has proposed becoming aware of and rejecting images of God as a warrior and images that present God as looking like an "aging male human of European heritage." We have endorsed images that perceive a comparison with God in the loving, creative, healing, joyful, spiritual, and physical actions of human beings.

Reflection Questions

1. To what extent do you agree that images of God as a warrior should be eliminated from Christian theology and practice?

2. Describe your level of comfort with the idea that we must be selective in preserving some biblical images of God rather than others.

3. Why does "Lord" appeal to you as a title for the one God? Or why does it not appeal?

Chapter Nine

Father and Mother of Us All

God was occasionally compared to a merciful father in the Jewish Scriptures, but not as often as some people might think: fewer than ten times in the Hebrew Bible, and only in Psalms, Isaiah, and Jeremiah.

> You, O LORD, are our father;
>   our Redeemer from of old is your name. (Isaiah 63:16)
>
> O LORD, you are our Father;
>   we are the clay, and you are our potter;
>   we are all the work of your hand. (Isaiah 64:8)
>
> I thought you would call me, My Father,
>   and would not turn from following me. (Jeremiah 3:19)
>
> As a father has compassion for his children,
> so the LORD has compassion for those who fear him.
>   (Psalm 103:13)

The last citation above begins to express some of the ambivalence implied in the title "father." God is spoken of as a father who is compassionate toward those who fear God. Fathers in those ancient times were the embodiment of the term "patriarch."

They were the heads of their households; their wives and children were considered their property; they gave orders and expected them to be strictly obeyed. We can redefine the word "fear" in these more moderate times to mean respect or reverence, but in the days when the psalms were written, "fear" was an apt description, and a "compassionate father" would be a contradiction in terms in most cases. Still, at least once in the Hebrew Scriptures, God is described as a compassionate father.

"Father" was surely the most important image of God for Jesus. He taught his followers to pray to God as "our Father." In the Gospel of John, in particular, he refers repeatedly to his mission from his Father and constantly speaks of God as "your heavenly Father."

Mark's gospel reports that in a remarkable moment of intimacy, as Jesus prayed fearfully in the garden the evening before his death, he addressed God as *Abba*. The Aramaic word *Abba* was a familiar term used by those who were emotionally close, including even adult children when addressing their father; it was also used to express a relationship characterized by esteem and confidence. Jesus' prayer to his *Abba* at the most vulnerable moment of his life, as he confronted the prospect of death, is profoundly moving in its tenderness and trust.

The image of God as Father has endured through centuries of human experience as a profound expression of the faithfulness and loving-kindness of God. Still, the image of God as father, like all the other images, is both valuable and ambivalent. In the closing decades of the twentieth century we became ever more profoundly aware of how badly the image of fatherhood has been corrupted by human sinfulness, both by male parents and by clergy who are called "Father." When that corruption has been experienced at the emotional level, no amount of talking can overcome the damage. It is far from supportive to tell abused women or children that God is like their father. We must be able to express the reality of God's love to them through other imagery. At the same time, since fathers at their best are benevolent, we should retain the image of God as the best of fathers.

For some believers it may be helpful to supplement the "father" image with others. A version of the Lord's Prayer developed by a Maori Christian community in New Zealand and incorporated in the Anglican Church of New Zealand's prayer book paraphrases the opening invocation as "Eternal Spirit, Earth-maker, Pain-bearer, Life-giver, Source of all that is and shall be, Father and Mother of us all, Loving God in whom is heaven . . . ." That opening phrase uses seven images of God in addition to "our father." All of them are valuable for reflection and prayer.

God as Mother

We will select one of those images for further discussion immediately: the image of God as Mother.

> The Rock, his work is perfect,
>   and all his ways are just.
> A faithful God, without deceit,
>   just and upright is he. (Deuteronomy 32:4)
>
> The Lord is my rock, my fortress, and my deliverer,
>   my God, my rock in whom I take refuge. (Psalm 18:2)
>
> Rock of ages, cleft for me . . . (traditional hymn)

Although both biblical and Christian tradition have considered it appropriate to think of God as a *rock*, many traditional believers are opposed to thinking of God as a mother! "A rock is only a symbol," some believers point out; "we're not saying that God *is* a rock, but that God is reliable like a shelter made of rock." Agreed—but "mother" is "only a symbol," too—and so is "father." We should use all the images that tell us something valid about God, recognizing that all are images and that each therefore speaks imperfectly about the spiritual reality who is God.

In fact, the Scriptures do occasionally portray God as a mother, giving birth to the people, nursing her children at the breast, lifting her child up to her cheek, teaching her child to walk.

As a mother comforts her child,
   so will I comfort you. (Isaiah 66:13; see also Isaiah 42:14,
      where God cries out like a woman in labor.)

Can a woman forget her nursing child,
   or show no compassion for the child of her womb?
Even these may forget,
   yet I will not forget you. (Isaiah 49:15)

The eagle in the famous modern hymn is a mother eagle, teaching her eaglets to fly by carrying them skyward on her back, tipping them off into thin air, and diving to rescue any offspring that cannot achieve airworthiness.

You have seen . . . how I bore you on eagles' wings and brought you to myself. (Exodus 19:4)

Once (Hosea 13:8) God is even compared to a mother bear protecting her young.

Holy Spirit is sometimes perceived as the "feminine principle" in our understanding of God. The word for "spirit" in both Hebrew and Greek is feminine; grammatically any pronoun in English about the Spirit should be feminine. Perhaps evolving our language of prayer to take that into account would be helpful for some. But "God is neither male nor female," and gender-exclusive pronouns *of either gender* are problematic.

Although God has never been addressed as "our Mother" in the Hebrew or Christian Scriptures or in traditional prayer, we have seen that God is described by several images of maternal love in the Bible. We should all appreciate the beauty of those feminine images of our God.

God loves us as our Creator, our Redeemer, and our Savior. God loves us like the best of fathers; God loves us like the best of mothers.

Conscious Gender Neutrality in Speaking of God

The next chapter will be entirely positive in discussing the idea
that God is Spirit. This chapter will conclude with more necessary
critical comments about past and current practice. We have spoken already of several problematic images of God that are concrete or "human-like" (old man, warrior, king). To emphasize the
spiritual nature of God, especially in speaking with children, we
should make a conscious effort to avoid inappropriate imagery
in talking about God. For example, only bodily beings have gender; there is no male or female in spiritual reality. Gender-exclusive language is to be avoided in talking about God. An exception
should be made for the classic image of Father, as long as the
image of Mother is at least occasionally mentioned. But King and
Master are exclusively images of dominant males and should be
used as infrequently as possible. The same is true of the ubiqui-
tous "Lord," especially in the phrase "Lord of Hosts," with its
warrior connotations. A lord is always male. The God who spoke
to Moses and who sent Jesus is not male. God is Spirit.

In recent decades translators and musicians have made significant efforts to reduce gender-exclusive language in readings
and hymns. A particularly vexing problem is the gendered nature
of pronouns in the English language. The words *son* and *sa* in
French can mean either "his" or "her"—they do not specify gender. Also, in many languages, including Hebrew and Greek, the
verb includes the pronoun; the pronoun is often not even written
separately from the verb. When a Hebrew verb like *bara* (creates)
is translated into English we have to use a pronoun: *he/she/it*
"creates." The result is that we have come to use "he" when referring to God, and the masculine imagery is perpetuated.

There are only a few partial solutions: Awkward as it may feel,
try to use the gender-neutral word "God" instead of a masculine
pronoun as often as possible. In hymns and psalms, change
masculine pronouns to "you"—a word that is gender-neutral.
(Often the psalms themselves literally move from second- to
third-person pronouns in consecutive verses. Stay with second
person throughout!) Instead of male-exclusive titles (Lord, King,

Master), choose words or phrases that do not refer to gender: Creator, Savior, Redeemer—or, of course, simply "God."

The issue of language is significant, as the Roman Catholic Church's leadership well knows. The Vatican has systematically *rejected* the use of gender-neutral language in translations of church documents. In their language, God still wills to save all men. Vatican translators have even produced such a sentence as "God speaks intimately, as one man to another."[1]

What is proposed in this chapter is undeniably a revolutionary shift in language usage with the purpose of promoting more accurate and credible thinking about God. The time has come to make the necessary changes, at least in our personal thinking and language.

Reflection Questions

1. Reflect on and express what the image of God as Father means to you.

2. Reflect on and express what the image of God as Mother means to you.

3. Why might the image of father be troublesome for some people? What should the community do to respond to their concerns?

4. What is your reaction to the proposed use of (a) gender-neutral and (b) feminine images in speaking about God?

5. How forceful should we be in working toward fully inclusive language in speaking about God?

[1] In Benedict XVI, *Jesus of Nazareth*, large print ed. (New York: Random House, 2007), chap. 4, "The Sermon on the Mount," 124.

Chapter Ten

God Is Spirit

For many people (and perhaps especially children) of the twenty-first century the only certain reality is what is concrete and measurable and scientifically proven. We live in what seems to be a material world, and we tend to think that only what we can see and hear, or what we can demonstrate and prove, is real. We have become programmed by our culture to look at life superficially. If people's—and especially children's—lives are limited to the measurable world, they will be tragically unaware of the real and far more powerful spiritual world.

Earlier in this book humans were described as body-beings capable of spiritual activity. Human behavior in the spiritual realm includes our ability to reflect on and evaluate our own behavior and experiences, to abstract and conceptualize, to communicate by language and art, to decide on the basis of a wide variety of factors, and to *imagine*—in a way, to live inwardly in other times and places. And of course we can believe, and get in touch with God in prayer. We can explore the possible outcomes of our future actions, we can experience the life conditions under which people existed in the past, or we can be drawn into the imaginary world of a novel. Our language and art seem far more sophisticated than those of any other known inhabitants of our planet. Many people believe we can communicate with others, living or even dead, in a way that is "extrasensory."

Such activities are properly described as spiritual, though they are activities of our brain. The spiritual realm is real; it is powerful in the sense that it can change lives and indeed can change the world. It is beyond the reach of measurement or scientific proof.

Believers understand that God is a spiritual reality, and that the various physical images that have been used for God must be understood as symbols that point to a spiritual reality. We must find ways of expressing the reality and value of the spiritual realm that are believable, particularly to our children. Even the smallest children must be taught that God is Spirit, and that spiritual reality is just as real as what they see on television.

In the ensuing sections of this chapter we will present ways of describing the action of God by using spiritual language.

Images of the Spirit of God

Wind

> The wind [or: the Spirit] blows where it chooses, and you hear the sound of it, but you do not know where it comes from or where it goes. (John 3:8)

The main problem for both adults and children in talking about God as a spiritual reality is that everyone seems to think of spirit as invisible and inert, like the air—real and important, to be sure, but hard to "get hold of," hard to describe. In what follows, try to understand the word Spirit to mean both the Holy Spirit and the spiritual reality we call God (the one God, the God who spoke to Moses, the God to whom Jesus prayed, and the Spirit sent by Jesus to lead us into all truth).

The key to making believable statements about God as Spirit is to think in terms of energy, power, and action. *God is more like the wind than the still air.* If you have ever been caught in a hurricane or tornado or just a windstorm, or if you have played a sport on a windy day, or walked in the canyons between skyscrapers, you know what it means to be pushed somewhere by an invisible power that is in control of you. That is the image evoked by John's gospel in the quotation above: an unseen energy, a power of which it must be said that you do not know where it comes from or where it is going—but an invisible power that can control you.

Wind as a symbol of the powerful presence of God resonates deeply within human consciousness. Images of God as a powerful wind are found from the first page of the Bible to the book of Job to the narrative of Pentecost to the Gospel of John. In fact, the same word [*ruach* in Hebrew, *pneuma* in Greek] can be translated as either "wind" or "spirit," and most correctly as both at once. "Wind" provides a sensory symbol we have experienced; "spirit" is what is symbolized.

> The earth was a formless void and darkness covered the face of the deep, while a wind from God [or: the Spirit of God] swept over the face of the waters. (Genesis 1:2)
>
> Then [God] answered Job out of the whirlwind. (Job 38:1)
>
> And suddenly from heaven there came a sound like the rush of a violent wind, and it filled the entire house where they were sitting. . . . All of them were filled with the Holy Spirit . . . (Acts 2:2, 4)

In the Acts of the Apostles, after being engulfed by the Spirit of God, Peter goes forth to proclaim the good news of Jesus. Everyone in the crowd understands what Peter is saying, though they speak a wide variety of languages. The scene is deliberately presented as the reversal of the story of the Tower of Babel: in that symbolic narrative (Genesis 11:1-9) the variety of languages on earth is portrayed as the consequence of human sinfulness.

Sin establishes barriers to human communication and together-ness. At Pentecost the powerful Spirit of God overcomes the barriers of language and brings people together in love. Every-one can understand. The Spirit that is God is a spirit of action. The Spirit transforms human lives.

Fire

Fire is another biblical image of the spiritual reality we call God. When Moses experienced his history-changing conversion in the Sinai desert (Exodus 3), the presence of God was described by the image of a fire that did not consume the bush where it resided. While the Israelites wandered for forty years in the desert they were led by God in the form of a pillar of fire by night (Exodus 13:21-22). When the friends of Jesus were trans-formed by the Spirit of God from frightened cowards to inspi-rational evangelists, tongues as of fire rested on their heads (Acts 2:3). To signify the presence of the risen Jesus in the Easter season we light the paschal candle; candles are used throughout the liturgical year to signify the presence of the divine.

Fire, like wind, is a primordial symbol of the presence of God. It resonates in our hearts and speaks to us in a way words can-not. Nonetheless, we have to use words to try to express the significance of fire as an image of God. Formulaic explanations about illumination or purifying have a truth, but they do not captivate the human soul.

But think about fire. Is it really there? If it is, why can I run a solid object through the flame as if it was not there? Of course it is there, and it is real and powerful, but it is very hard to get hold of. We cannot define its dimensions; we cannot capture it. In many ways, though physical, it is almost spiritual. We can sit and look at a fire for ages, meditating or just emptying our minds. It is always changing; it is always the same.

Fire is powerful and dangerous. It can destroy anything we have built, can totally change the circumstances of our lives, and can even kill. We have to be respectful of fire; we must not take it lightly or act as if it is not there. If we do, we are likely to bring harm on ourselves.

And fire is vibrant and transforming. There is energy in a log, but the energy is inert. When fire takes possession of a log, that inert energy takes life and dances off into the air. The log is transformed into heat and light.

Can you see why fire has always been an image of the presence of God? God is real; God is Spirit; God is always the same, yet always doing new things. We must respect God; we must not take God lightly or act as if God is not there. If we do not pay attention to God we bring harm on ourselves. If the Spirit of God takes possession of us, we will be transformed and made more vibrant. Can you feel why fire expresses the presence of God in a way that goes beyond words?

The Actions of the Spirit of God

> The Spirit of [God] shall rest on him,
> the Spirit of wisdom and understanding,
> the Spirit of counsel and might,
> the Spirit of knowledge and fear of [God] . . . (Isaiah 11:2)

Chapter 11 of the book of the prophet Isaiah begins with a hopeful description of what God will do for the Messiah: God's Spirit will make the Anointed One wise, reverent, astute. We Christians have extended its meaning, adapting Isaiah's confident hope under the title "gifts of the Holy Spirit." Thus we teach our young people at the sacrament of confirmation that God will do for them what God promised to do for the Messiah.

Believe this: The Spirit-God ignites us, helps us to be wise, to make sense out of our lives, to have reverence for the greatness of God, to make good choices, and to have the courage to do what we know is right. Reflect on each of those phrases, one at a time. This is what God offers us. Wisdom, understanding, reverence, true perspective, right judgment, courage, a sense of awe and wonder—these are all spiritual characteristics of a mature human person. And they are all gifts of a God whose action is always to inspire us to learn from our experiences, to understand the direction of our lives, to make decisions that are both honest and wise, to live courageously, and to recognize the role God can play in our lives and in our world. We can rely on God to lead us to wholeness in all these ways if we are willing to open our hearts to God's powerful spiritual action within us.

> The Spirit of . . . God is upon me . . .
> [God] has sent me to bring good news to the oppressed,
> to bind up the brokenhearted,
> to proclaim liberty to the captives,
> and release to the prisoners,
> to proclaim the year of [God's] favor . . .
> (Isaiah 61:1-2, quoted by Jesus in Luke 4:18)

When Jesus inaugurated his mission, according to the Gospel of Luke, he read that passage from Isaiah in his hometown synagogue and then told the congregation that those words were being fulfilled as he spoke.

Jesus believed that the spiritual action of God is to help people to be free, no matter what the circumstances of their lives. From the time when the Hebrew people were led forth into freedom under Moses, God has been known as the One who stands for liberty—freedom from what oppresses us, freedom to direct our lives toward wholeness. God's action will never be a magical elimination of all the hardships of life, but God offers to help us in our inner lives to deal with the routine and joy and tension and sadness of life—to "bind up the brokenhearted."

Luke 4:18 (where Jesus quotes Isaiah's description of the action of the Spirit of God in support of the poor and oppressed) is invoked as the focus of their activities by many Christian groups devoted to action in support of social justice. Much of our discussion of wholeness was oriented toward individual growth, but an unmistakable element of personal growth is self-giving, loving communal action. No one can claim to be wise, or to be a faithful disciple of Jesus, without being deeply concerned for and taking action to support the well-being of others.

In the first section of this book the point about the importance of social involvement was made especially in the chapter on living our values consistently. In this section dealing with the spiritual action of God in our lives, the point must be reemphasized: The Spirit of God is available for us to push us like a powerful wind, to ignite us to take action to bring good news to the oppressed, to set prisoners free (from whatever imprisons them), and to bring about the reign of God in our society. If we think the Spirit of God acts to help us become whole without being involved in the struggles of other people in our world, we just are not listening to the sound of the mighty Wind. If we do listen, with the help of God's spiritual power we can continue to grow toward wholeness, toward becoming the persons we are meant to be, toward peace of heart.

Reflection Questions

1. List some of your recent activities that you would describe as spiritual.

2. Reflect on and tell about your significant experiences with wind and fire. Express why they are good images of the presence of God.

3. Discuss some of the "gifts of the Holy Spirit" in terms of how God's action can help you to be wise, to understand the meaning of your life, to make good decisions, etc.

Chapter Eleven

God Is Love

One of the spiritual realities most children have experienced is love. Ask children whether love is real. They will assure you that it is.

Is love powerful? Certainly: children grow because of the power of the love that surrounds them. Without love, a child will shrivel and die. When you are older and someone says for the first time, "I love you," that love is powerful enough to change your whole life. You are a new person. When "I love you" is repeated endlessly you are affirmed and continue to grow toward wholeness because of the power of love. The same is true in the opposite way if someone says, "I don't love you any more." You are shattered; you are not yourself any more; your growth toward wholeness is hindered.

Love is also powerful in the sense that it is creative and redemptive and transforming. Humans come to be as the result of an act that is called "making love." Love is healing: forgiving a wrong that has been done to you heals and transforms both yourself and the person who is being forgiven. Your love for each other becomes stronger if the gift of forgiveness is received with a whole heart.

Where is love? It is within us and within everyone; it is all around us; it is everywhere in the world. How old is love? It has been around as long as there have been people, and it will last for as long as people continue to live.

The New Testament makes the simple declaration that God is love:

> God is love, and those who abide in love abide in God, and
> God abides in them. (1 John 4:16)

Like love, God is a spiritual reality. Like love, God is real and powerful, within us, all around us, and forever. With children we must use words of fewer syllables to express our belief that God is creative, redemptive, and transforming love.

Is love "concrete" or physical? Can you measure love (or God) scientifically or capture it in a bottle? Of course not, because love is spiritual. If you think that only the measurable is real you have neglected a very important element of human experience.

> I have loved you with an everlasting love;
>
> therefore I have continued my faithfulness to you.
> (Jeremiah 31:3)

The idea that God loves people "with an everlasting love" is one of the most distinctive features of our biblical tradition. No other religion I know of speaks of the relationship between God and people as one of mutual love. "You shall love . . . your God with all your heart, and with all your soul, and with all your might" (Deuteronomy 6:4) has been part of the daily prayer of the Jewish people for more than three thousand years. A scroll with those words on it can be found inside the little box you may have noticed on the doorposts of the homes of devout Jewish people still today. Jesus (and many other rabbis before him) identified that teaching as the greatest commandment in the Law of Moses. You may have noticed that it is not one of the Ten Commandments, but part of the larger Law of Moses that includes a total of 613 commandments: the greatest commandment is not one of the ten.

The love of God is repeatedly linked in the Bible with God's fidelity. From the beginning of their religious history the Jewish people have known what it means to belong to God. The Bible's most important term for the bond between God and the people is "covenant." We are invited to feel chosen or adopted as God's children, just as those first liberated slaves were given a new sense of themselves as people who are cared for, who belong, who are loved.

> You have seen . . . how I bore you on eagles' wings and brought you to myself. Now therefore, if you obey my voice and keep my covenant, you shall be my treasured possession out of all the peoples. (Exodus 19:5)

A classic phrase endlessly repeated in the Bible to describe the action of God is "steadfast love and faithfulness."

> . . . a God merciful and gracious,
> slow to anger,
> and abounding in steadfast love and faithfulness,
> keeping steadfast love for the thousandth generation.
> (Exodus 34:6-7)
>
> . . . as the heavens are high above the earth,
> so great is [God's] steadfast love toward those who fear
>   him;
>
> . . .
>
> As a father has compassion for his children,
> so [God] has compassion for those who fear him.
> (Psalm 103:11, 13)

Most Christians have been taught the stereotype that the God of Moses was judgmental and vengeful, but a thoughtful reading of the Hebrew Scriptures reveals the contrary: the Jewish people knew God as a God of "steadfast love" who constantly loves and forgives the wayward human community. The word currently translated as "steadfast love" is one of the most frequently repeated phrases in the Hebrew Scriptures. It recurs literally hundreds of times and certainly confirms that the Hebrews knew God as a God of love. The phrase in Hebrew (*ḥesed wᵉemeth*) is composed of two nouns, one meaning "loving-kindness" and the other meaning "fidelity." Those are the primary characteristics of God as revealed to the Hebrews. They are stunning words: no other religion or civilization ever considered its gods as acting toward the people with "loving-kindness and fidelity." It is so unprecedented that it makes one believe this attribute of God can truly be considered "revealed by God." It seems unlikely that human beings "invented" the idea that "God is love." It is credible to believe that God revealed this understanding in the course of nurturing the Jewish community.

This belief in a God of love is one of the most treasured aspects of the faith we have inherited from the Jewish tradition: God loves each of us as we are, without conditions. God is faithful; God can be trusted. God offers to lead us toward wholeness so that we can become "who we really are" in the course of our life journey. And God invites us to respond by loving God at the depths of our being and in everything we do.

God is love. This idea is the key to teaching children about God as a spiritual reality, so that they will not have to unlearn the more physical images of God that have customarily been given to them. How can we convey this beautiful spiritual understanding of God to children? Follow the same line of thinking about God that was followed about love in this chapter: Love is not in some place in the sky, but is within us, and within everyone else, and all around us, forever in the past and forever into the future. Love is real and powerful; love creates us; love transforms us; love sets us free; love heals us. Repeat these phrases, substituting "God" for "love," and children may begin to understand something about the spiritual reality who is God.

When children inevitably ask, "Where is God?" the best way to answer is to return the question: "Where is love?"

Ask a child to draw a picture of love, and you surely will not be given a picture of an old man sitting on a throne. You may get a heart, or two people embracing, or a parent and child, or people holding hands, or someone visiting a loved one in the hospital. Ask the child if the drawing of a heart "shows what love looks like," and most likely the child will understand that the heart is a *symbol* of love, not a realistic picture of love. Why can we not do something similar about God? God does not look like an old man. God is love, and any symbolic representation of the reality of love helps us understand what God is like.

On the basis of this attempted refocusing of our language about God around the ideas of spirit and love we will later in this book try to respond to the grief-stricken question, "If God is love, how can God allow this terrible event that has shattered my life and left me questioning my faith? Why doesn't God prevent bad things from happening to good people?"

Before discussing that vital question, however, let us offer other credible and valuable statements we can make about the God we know as spirit and love.

Reflection Questions

1. What does it mean to you to say that God is love? (Don't consider the associated problems: we haven't gotten to those issues yet.)

Chapter Twelve

God Is Our Savior and Redeemer

Do not fear, for I have redeemed you;
  I have called you by name, you are mine.
For I am the Lord your God, the Holy One of Israel,
  your Savior.

(Isaiah 43:1, 3)

Isaiah proclaims that God redeems us and saves us. "God redeems" means that God frees us to set the course of our life in pursuit of wholeness. "God saves us" means "God reaches into our lives and leads us to wholeness."

The first section of this book described some of the elements of human wholeness, which all of us are seeking on our lifelong journey. The religious component of our quest for wholeness is the saving action of God. "Wholeness" and "salvation" are parallel terms for the goal of our life-journey. Exploring the concept of wholeness enables us to describe the person we are growing toward. Salvation is what *God* can do for us—God leads us toward wholeness. The good news of our faith tradition is that we do not have to strive to achieve wholeness on our own: the spiritual power of God is with us, giving us the energy to live our lives in love, enabling us to be wise and courageous. That is the essential meaning of the word "salvation." Salvation is not something that happens to us after we die; God's spiritual power is saving us *now*, in the course of our daily lives. (In the last chapter of this book we will talk about our hope for life beyond death as the last result of God's saving action.)

The Jewish people knew God as their Savior from the beginning of God's self-revelation to them. For the Jewish people (and indeed also in the gospels), the saving action of God is never understood as God's response to the sin of Adam and Eve. The "original sin" narrative expresses the insight of an author who was struggling to reconcile his belief in the loving-kindness of God with the existence of hardship and tragedy in the world. His insight (presented by means of a story) is that the evil that exists in the world is "not God's fault": God made the world out of love; people wrecked God's world by their sinfulness. The hardships we suffer, said this author, are the consequences of our sinfulness. Later books in the Hebrew Scriptures (such as Job) challenged his insight, declaring that our hardships should not be understood as punishment from God for our sins. No later book in the Hebrew Scriptures even mentions the sin of Adam and Eve.

As the Hebrew Scriptures understand human experience, history is the narrative of God's generous initiative, reaching out to people to lead them to wholeness. God "redeemed" the Hebrews (see Exodus 6:6) by setting them free from the slave camps in Egypt, simply because God wished to help them. Earlier we discussed the importance of freedom as an element of wholeness. The Jewish people have always known God as fundamentally "the God who sets us free."

God "saved" them means that God formed a covenant with the community: they belong to God; they are God's people. They learned that God loves people and invites people to love God in return. The Hebrew Scriptures are quite in tune with the New Testament proclamation that God is love. The daily prayer of the Jewish people for millennia has been:

> Hear, O Israel: the Lord is our God; the Lord alone. You shall
> love the LORD your God with all your heart, and with all your
> soul, and with all your might. (Deuteronomy 6:4)

Further saving actions of God include the gift of the Law to guide their steps as faithful people of God. And God, while known as demanding, was also known to be forgiving, faithfully loving the people and never abandoning them in spite of their failings. In everything God is revealed to be acting to help us, and in no way acting against us. With God's help we can grow toward wholeness.

Jesus' proclamation of the saving love of God was expressed in terms of the "reign of God." Jesus followed the religion of Moses and proclaimed that the saving action of God was continuing in his life. Christians later gave to Jesus the title of Savior that had been used only for the action of God in bringing wholeness to the Jewish community. Christians believe that Jesus was sent by God to be Savior of the entire human family.

Jesus invited his followers to accept the reign of God in their lives. "If you will let God rule your heart," he announced, "God will transform you and lead you to wholeness." All the teaching of Jesus and all his deeds (including his death and resurrection) are dedicated to leading us toward wholeness. It might be useful at this stage to return to the section on "What Makes Us Whole," review what is needed for us to achieve wholeness, and consider how the spiritual energy of God can contribute to each of those elements. Our faith is Good News. We can rely on God to bring about this wonderful result in our lives.

Christians have long understood Jesus to be God's greatest gift to humanity. We believe that in the life of Jesus, God was among us in a way that has never happened before or since. To express that belief we declare that Jesus is Son of God.

Traditionally, the death of Jesus has been seen as the decisive saving event in his ministry. Consider also the saving value of *everything* Jesus did. His *teaching* saves us by helping us to realize that God offers to transform us, and by offering his wisdom about a way of living that is truly best for us. His *healings* were not only for the benefit of the people who were healed; they also assure us of the transforming power of God's reign. In some way *we* are the persons who are healed: we are blind, though our eyes may work; we are the outcasts, victims of oppression in ways only we know in our hearts; we are crippled and we need to "walk the talk"; our hands do not work as well as they might to bring service and comfort to others; we have gone through symbolic death at times in our lives, and we look forward to new life before we die. If we see only the symptoms in the healings of Jesus, we have missed their central purpose: Jesus' healings show us that God is willing to transform us as God transformed the lives of suffering people through the actions of Jesus. "Jesus saves us" also by his *lifestyle*—the way he lived as a poor preacher, associating with outcasts and challenging oppressive wealth and corrupt authority.

The *death of Jesus* should not be seen as "paying God back for the insult of Adam's sin," but as profoundly summing up Jesus' whole life: as God's greatest gift, Jesus gave his life, from birth to death, in the service of humanity, as an expression of his integrity and as a gift of love.

When he rose to new life he was vindicated. His *resurrection* shows that God was with Jesus in everything he did. Through the saving life of Jesus, God offers to transform us. Further, resurrection is not just something that happened to Jesus, but resurrection is also saving for us: Jesus lives now in a new way; he lives as God lives; he is within us and all around us, making us whole, giving us the spiritual energy to live in love, to be wise, to be courageous, to do what is true.

This is what it means to say that Jesus lived, died, and rose to save us. His life, death, and resurrection are a continuation of God's saving action, taking the initiative to reach into human life and lead us to wholeness.

Reflection Questions

1. Express in your own words the role of God's and Jesus' saving power in leading us toward wholeness:

    (a) an awareness of being loved

    (b) a sense of purpose

    (c) a consistent personal value system

    (d) freedom

    (e) emotional well-being and intimacy

Chapter Thirteen

The Forgiving God
and the Meaning of Sin

[God] does not deal with us according to our sins,
nor repay us according to our iniquities.
For as the heavens are high above the earth,
so great is [God's] steadfast love toward those who fear
[God];
as far as the east is from the west,
so far [God] removes our transgressions from us.

(Psalm 103:10-12)

What Does It Mean to Sin?

On the personal level sin is a free, deliberate choice to do something one knows to be wrong. Each of the terms in that definition deserves some explanation.

Sin should be taken seriously. It should be recognized for what it is when it occurs, but it is not something trivial or superficial. It does not happen "automatically" when someone does something considered to be wrong. Many believers have a regrettably superficial understanding of sin because they began to learn about sin when they were little children and have never developed a sense of sin that is worthy of mature adults. Many were required to accept the sacrament of forgiveness at a time in their lives when they were told that telling a lie, or disobeying their parents, or using vulgar language was sinful. Many, at least in the older generations, "invented" sins to tell the priest when they were taken to the sacrament as a group. Many have never been taught that it is possible to act against the teaching of God and the church and not commit sin. To be a sin, a deed must include certain required subjective elements.

To commit sin, a person must be free. Any factor that reduces a person's freedom reduces guilt. Freedom may be reduced by any number of circumstances, perhaps including childhood deprivation, cultural traditions, inadequate instruction, social pressure, addiction, habit, oppression, or force. One of Jesus' challenging teachings is that no observer is entitled to judge the motivation or guilt of anyone else. "Do not judge, so that you may not be judged" (Matthew 7:1). Only God can comprehend all the factors that may have contributed to a person's actions. Only God is entitled to judge.

To be sinful, a choice must be deliberate. We must help our children understand that no one can sin by accident; one can only sin on purpose. If harm results from an unintentional deed, the deed may be regrettable, but it is not sinful. An action is not a sin just because you were punished for doing it, or because someone shouted at you because of what you did. It is only a sin if you make a free, deliberate choice.

The sinner must also be aware that the action is wrong. The moral teaching of our tradition should be understood as wisdom: Jesus challenges us to do the best we can, to be as true to ourselves and as faithful to God as we possibly can in the course of our journey toward wholeness. Sin is not about breaking laws; it is about failing to do what one realizes one should do. "Anyone . . . who knows the right thing to do and fails to do it, commits sin" (James 4:17). In a way, this understanding makes sin more present in our lives: it is not about crossing lines or "trespassing"; it is about falling short of the mark. In another way, many actions that may have been considered sinful in the past may not be sins at all. The responsible decision to contravene a law in the name of a greater good (for example, unlawful nonviolent protest actions), or the decision to do what one considers to be right despite traditional teaching (for example, remarriage after divorce), are possible examples.

Such decisions may in fact be wrong; there really is a moral truth to seek in every decision. An American cultural icon, Bob Dylan, is frequently quoted as having said that "the truth is true," whether one wants to believe it or not, and that the notion that each person has his or her own truth is a lie that has done a great deal of damage. Church leaders are convinced of the truth of the moral wisdom they proclaim, and they also respect the responsibility of believers to make decisions. The honest dissenter may be mistaken but may not necessarily be sinning in making such choices.

In a sophisticated document republished repeatedly over many years, the Roman Catholic bishops of Ontario, Canada, wrote: "Human understanding of God's will is often imperfect, so it can happen that *someone who acts against the teaching of God and the Church, even in serious matters, may not be committing sin.* One may not have 'sufficient knowledge,' and one's sense of values may not be sufficiently developed to be fully responsible for one's actions. Moreover, immaturity, psychological imbalance and habit can also diminish freedom and hence the deliberate character of an act, so that it is not always a serious fault."[1]

In that document the bishops refer to the example of married couples who decide that their family circumstances justify the use of contraceptive technology to prevent the birth of a child. The bishops consider two cases: people who disagree with Catholic teaching on this issue and people who *agree* with the

---

[1] "Human Sexuality and the Will of God," in *Guidelines for Family Life Education* (Toronto: The Ontario Conference of Catholic Bishops: 1977, 1983, 1987), 42.1. Italics supplied.

Catholic teaching in principle but consider that their particular circumstances cause a "clear conflict of duties" for them. "In accord with the accepted principles of moral theology," the bishops write, quoting the official Canadian response to *Humanae Vitae* in 1968, "if these persons have tried sincerely but without success to pursue a line of conduct in keeping with the given directives, they may be safely assured that *whoever honestly chooses that course which seems right, does so in good conscience.*"[2] The bishops agree with the pope's teaching, and they consider the couple's decision to be mistaken and wrong, but they do not accuse such people of sin, though the couple has chosen to do something that contravenes Catholic teaching.

That teaching about the role of personal conscience in decision making must be balanced by a strong presentation of the objective validity of traditional teaching. In fact, the same bishops make both points, side by side, in the quoted document. "This statement [the previously-quoted sentence on respect for personal conscience] cannot be understood as lessening the full force of the Church's teaching. The teaching of the *magisterium* [the teaching authority of the church] cannot be just one element among others in the formation of conscience. A believer has the absolute obligation of conforming [his or her] conscience first and foremost to what the Church teaches. . . . For a Catholic, 'to follow one's conscience' is not, then, simply to act as unguided reason dictates."[3]

Those paragraphs are surprising, and indeed seriously confusing to many believing adults who have been taught that certain actions are always or "automatically" sinful. The fact that a conference of bishops has published such almost-contradictory statements side by side is an indication that there is truth on both sides of the discussion. The bishops' teaching is sophisticated and respectful of adult believers. They point out that it is the centuries-old teaching of moral theologians and of the teach-

[2] Ibid., 59.
[3] Ibid., 60.

ing authority of the Catholic Church. The Canadian document was approved in a letter to the bishops by the pope, who agreed that it appropriately applies the universal teaching to the needs of the national church. It respects the right of believers to make responsible decisions in good conscience even when they disagree with traditional teaching. At the same time, it reaffirms the importance of being guided by the official teaching of the church.

Part of the human quest for wholeness is the search for truth. We must be honest with ourselves; we must consider the wisdom of our tradition and seriously face the truth as we make our decisions. At the same time, we have been given the gift of freedom. We are responsible for our decisions. We have the right to choose to do what we honestly consider to be good or justifiable or the best possible under the circumstances.

Sin is a free, deliberate choice to do something that one knows to be wrong. The discussion in the preceding paragraphs is about personal sin. The discerning believer must also be aware of "social sin." This is a challenging and perhaps unsolvable dilemma: to what extent am I guilty of the sins of my society? Even relatively poor citizens in the Western world live in comfort and wealth compared to the vast majority of the human family. We of the middle class use an outlandish share of the world's resources; we pollute our environment; our generosity to the deprived is a tiny portion of our excess wealth. Some of us complain when exploitative companies pay offshore workers ridiculously small wages, but often we are objecting because those companies are taking jobs away from our economy and giving them to workers in faraway places.

We do bear guilt for the evildoings of our civilization, but how it can be overcome is much harder to state. We still have to live in our society. We cannot follow literally Jesus' command to sell everything we have and give it to the poor. But we certainly should make an effort to use our wealth in the service of others and to take some kind of political action to reduce the damage we are doing as a group: refuse to buy products that are cheaper as the result of exploitation of workers; become aware of pollution and take steps to reduce it (reduce the use of machines that are fueled by petroleum and electricity; refuse to purchase foods imported from half a world away or to buy products that use excessive wrapping material); reuse and recycle products as much as possible. Such actions may be a route toward being forgiven for our part in the sins of our society.

To summarize this section on the meaning of sin: sin is a free, deliberate choice to do something we understand to be wrong. The common understanding of sin has become trivialized over the centuries, at least partly in an effort to instruct medieval peasants and twenty-first-century children. As a result many adults have not been given a mature understanding of our responsibility as decision makers, of the true seriousness of sin, and particularly of our complicity in social sin.

How is God Involved in Our Moral Journey?

The good news proclaimed in the Scriptures is that God is a spiritual power who acts to support us and is in no way against us. God loves humanity; God's action helps us to make sense of our lives, to freely set the course of our journey no matter what happens to us, to be wise, to make good decisions, to have the courage to do what we know is right. Our moral teaching, which we understand as wisdom from God, gives us insight about what kind of living will truly result in wholeness and peace of heart. We make our decisions in the context of a search for moral truth and in openness to the spiritual strength God offers as we pursue our quest for wholeness. But how does God respond to our failures and sinfulness?

Some parts of our tradition present a very humanlike portrait of a God who takes offense at what we do wrong, becomes angry and vengeful, "closes the gates of heaven," holds a grudge against humanity, requires retribution, and even demands the death of God's Son in recompense for the sins of humanity. Those ideas can be seen as the product of believers' reflection on their lives. They suffered endless misery; they recognized their sinfulness. The only way those believers could reconcile their belief in a loving God with the pain of their lives was to say that God is fair as well as loving. They understood their lifelong suffering as God's vengeance and punishment for their sins. The resulting understanding of God's role in human life is predictably negative. Jesus, however, did not see life's misery as God's punishment for sin. (See John 9:1-3.)

Many other parts of the biblical tradition present a very different understanding of God's response to our sins. The quotation at the beginning of this chapter declares that God responds to our sin with "steadfast love." Many other psalms speak of the forgiving God as well. Some of them are said to have been written by King David, who surely needed to be forgiven after having oppressed Bathsheba and murdered her husband to take possession of her. If David could believe that God had forgiven him, can we not believe that the steadfast love of God will forgive us also?

> Happy are those whose transgression is forgiven,
>   whose sin is covered.
> Happy are those to whom the Lord imputes no iniquity . . .
> (Psalm 32:1-2)

> Have mercy on me, O God,
>   according to your steadfast love;
> according to your abundant mercy
>   blot out my transgressions . . .
> Create in me a clean heart, O God,
>   and put a new and right spirit within me.
> (Psalm 51:1-2, 10)

> Out of the depths I cry to you, O Lord.
>   Lord, hear my voice! . . .
> If you, O Lord, should mark iniquities,
>   Lord, who could stand?
> But there is forgiveness with you,
>   so that you may be revered.
> (Psalm 130:1-4)

The entire book of the prophet Hosea is a reflection on the
forgiving nature of God. The beautiful chapter 11 summarizes
the spirit of the book in language that could bring to mind an
image of God as mother:

> When Israel was a child, I loved him,
>   and out of Egypt I called my son.
> The more I called them,
>   the more they went from me . . .
> Yet it was I who taught Ephraim to walk,
>   I took them up in my arms;
>   but they did not know that I healed them.
> I led them with cords of human kindness,
>   with bands of love.
> I was to them like those
>   who lift infants to their cheeks.
>   I bent down to them and fed them.
>   . . .
> How can I give you up, Ephraim?
>   How can I hand you over, O Israel? . . .
> My heart recoils within me;
>   my compassion grows warm and tender.
> I will not execute my fierce anger . . .
> for I am God and no mortal,
>   the Holy One in your midst,
>   and I will not come in wrath. (Hosea 11:1-9)

The teaching of Jesus about the forgiving nature of God is well
known. Many Christians believe it is the opposite of Jewish
teaching, but such is not the case. The Jewish tradition knew
God as faithful, loving, and forgiving. One contemporary rabbi
commented that no Jewish teacher ever taught that God would
sentence sinful believers to eternal damnation: "That's your
Jesus' teaching." So which tradition has the more vengeful image
of God? Unfortunately, some Christians continue to emphasize
the harsher aspects of Jesus' teaching about God in an effort to
challenge people to obey moral teaching. There is an undeniable
judgmental element in the teaching of Jesus, just as there is in

the Hebrew Scriptures, but in both testaments it is the forgiving and saving elements that predominate by far, and it is those teachings that must be appreciated and emphasized.

Traditional moral wisdom helps us to realize that when we sin we do harm to others, but we also harm *ourselves*. We hinder our own growth; we damage our own peace of heart; we impede our quest for wholeness. It is not that God "takes offense" at what we have done. It is that we have rejected, at least in part, God's offer of spiritual power to lead us toward wholeness. God does not reduce the flow of love toward us. We have resisted the saving action of God and diminished the energy of our relationship with God. We have harmed ourselves.

The joyful proclamation of the scriptural tradition is that the faithful love of God can overcome our failures. God's forgiveness is a wonderful gift. We do not have to go through life looking backward with regret. We can grow toward the future, knowing we are forgiven. We are always frail and wounded voyagers, but we believe that God is entirely on our side. Even when we sin, God is present as spiritual force, offering to heal us and restore our progress. It is important for us to recognize the truth about our actions: when we freely and deliberately harm others or act in a way that truly diminishes our growth toward wholeness, we are guilty of sin. To overcome our sin we must admit our failure and resume the journey—we must "ask God for forgiveness." Part of resuming the journey must be to ask forgiveness also of the person or persons we have injured and to restore justice as far as possible.

Somehow, in our own hearts, we must find a balance among several elements: the true nature of our call to wholeness and peace of heart, the radical and challenging moral teaching of Jesus, the saving energy offered by God, the honest evaluation of our actions, and the steadfast love of the forgiving God. No doubt there are times in most peoples' lives when we are simply not open to the wisdom of God. During those times some may even believe that they are doing well. The role of a church community (which may be as small as the people who gather around your kitchen table and as large as the worldwide Christian family) is to reach out, to challenge, to proclaim God's love, and to find ways to support each other. The journey continues. We are never alone.

It is essential to the ongoing journey that we open our hearts to the forgiving action of God, who overcomes our failures, heals our self-inflicted wounds, transforms us inwardly, and continues to lead us toward the wholeness we seek in our lifelong quest to become our truest selves.

Reflection Questions

1. What are the implications for your life of the teaching that sin is not something "automatic," but rather involves subjective elements (knowledge, freedom, deliberate choice), so that it is possible that a person could do something "wrong" and yet not sin?

2. Consider your personal responsibility for the evil done by communities (political, economic, and religious) to which you belong. What initiatives can we be expected to take to counteract the social sin in which we are complicit?

3. What helps you to believe in your heart that God forgives our sins?

4. It is very difficult to put aside traditional beliefs in a judgmental God, but try to express in your own words an entirely positive sense of God as being always on our side, giving us the spiritual power to grow toward wholeness, overcoming our failures, healing us, and leading us forward after we sin.

5. Explore the dynamic moral enterprise within you with regard to growing toward wholeness with God's spiritual help, falling short of what you know is best, recognizing and regretting shortcomings, overcoming failure, and continuing to make progress despite difficult circumstances.

Chapter Fourteen

God:
The Creator, Not the "Puppet Master"

The foregoing chapters have made a number of positive, beautiful statements about the spiritual action of God, who knows us and loves us for who we are and sets us free to be true to ourselves. God helps us to be wise and to make sense of our lives; God supports us as we try to make good choices and to have the courage to do what we know is right; God forgives us when we sin and offers to overcome our failures, heal us, and lead us ever onward toward wholeness.

Within that background perhaps we can begin again to consider some traditional statements about the action of God that call for reconsideration. It is important to reflect on all that we believe about God, reevaluate some traditional ideas as debatable, and continue to reaffirm our faith in what seems most credible for us.

One understanding about God is so familiar that it is almost taken for granted by many believers: the idea that God causes everything—or everything important—that happens in life.

Creation

Creation is best understood as an act of love. We understand our world and our lives as gifts of God, and we believe God imparts meaning to human life and to the universe. God is Creator, in some fundamental way the source of our being. Yet explanations about the interactions of causes in the universe are problematic. Human understanding feels its limitations when we try to explore causality, especially in this age of quantum physics and string theory.[1] We have the best chance of under-standing God's creation accurately if we leave to science the task of exploring demonstrable causes.

The stunning immensity of the universe and the amazing detail of the microscopic world inspire wonder in our hearts. In this remarkable time in human history we are taking pictures of parts of the universe as it looked eleven billion years ago. That is the meaning of a light year. Physicists tell us that it took eleven billion years for certain light rays to reach the Hubble telescope in its orbit and be recorded as a photograph. Now we can actu-ally see what part of the universe looked like, near its beginning. At the same time, we are mapping the human genome with formulas that exhaust the most powerful computers.

Our minds boggle when we try to imagine the source of this wonderment. We know that creation cannot be accurately com-pared to such human activities as an artist creating on canvas what is imagined in the mind or a computer programmer de-signing machines that calculate faster than any human. We feel our thinking is too limited when we imagine that God, like some immense computer, "figured out" the orbits of the stars and planets in billions of galaxies after the Big Bang or calculated the miniscule variations of DNA that distinguish one species from another. Still, those comparisons may be helpful for some searchers.

Creation must be infinitely more complicated than what we can understand when we make a statement such as "God made the world." Similarly, the network of causes that interplay in

---

[1] For a wiser discussion about modern science and its relationship to faith see chap. 4, "Science After Einstein," in Albert Nolan, OP, *Jesus Today* (Mary-knoll, NY: Orbis Books, 2006), 36–46.

our days and years is far too complex to be understood by a phrase like "God is the cause of everything that happens." Yet we feel that somehow God is the source of the immensity of the universe and the incredible variation, fecundity, and resilience of nature.

Perhaps the essential religious teaching about creation is that the world came to be as an act of love and is given to us as a gift. For me, creation is more credible when the concept refers to love and meaning rather than to causality. How does it affect me when I say that I understand my life as a gift to be lived in the embrace of the Spirit of Life?

God and Daily Events

Most believers realize that we do not correctly understand God's action in creation if we take the psalm literally when it says

> . . . I look at your heavens, the work of your fingers,
> the moon and the stars that you have established . . . .
> (Psalm 8:3)

Still, many of us do imagine that God causes everything that happens in our world, or that God is somewhat like a puppet master, pulling the strings that make people dance. It is difficult to express our misgivings about this traditional teaching in a way that is faithful, sensitive, and yet honest. But we must confront the question.

A case in point is the miracles of Jesus. If we spend our energy trying to ascertain the cause of those events we will never understand their purpose. Jesus was a healer, but he was not the only person in history who healed people in a way beyond what medicine could do. Not all of history's healers claimed to be true believers or channels of God's power. Some modern thinkers try to explain Jesus' miracles naturally, speculating, for example, that the healings were done by harnessing the mind-power of the healer and the patient, or that the multiplication of the loaves and fishes was a "miracle of sharing" rather than the creation of more food out of a small original supply. To me those speculations are not a problem for my faith; I think we are expending energy unnecessarily if we speculate on the cause of the healings. I am content to say that the cause of Jesus' healings is open for discussion or "unexplained." The *purpose* of the healings is what should be considered.

Jesus did not trust people who wanted to see more wonders but were not willing to accept the reign of God in their hearts (see Mark 8:11-12; John 2:23-24). He implied that if we focus on the symptoms we have missed the entire purpose of the miracle. If we fail to understand that in some way *we* are the persons who are healed, the miracles are literally meaningless for us. The point of the healing of the leper (Mark 1:40) is not just that Jesus cured a person's skin; it is that the reign of God can restore *our* wholeness by overcoming whatever dehumanization may afflict us because of the oppressive actions of others. The miracles of Jesus were intended to show us how God can transform our lives by spiritual power, giving us new vision (even though we think we can see), enabling us who have been spiritually crippled to "walk in his way," feeding our *spiritual* hunger at the deepest level of our being.

Bringing the discussion to the present: what is the role of God in the events of our world? We know that insurance companies ascribe natural disasters to "acts of God," but that idea contributes neither to an accurate description of the causes of the event nor to a valid understanding of God. We best understand causes if we confine ourselves to the observable. Tsunamis are natural events caused by the clash of tectonic plates; they are not the result of God's decision to end the lives of hundreds of thousands of people on a single afternoon.

Lightning is the result of the accumulation of positive and negative charges in the air and on the earth. If lightning strikes a tree in a nearby park, few people understand that event as the direct action of God. But if the tree falls on someone and causes fatal injuries, or if lightning strikes and kills one golfer among a foursome walking down a fairway, many believers revert to language indicating that God decided to spare the survivors and to "call the deceased person home." We console ourselves with phrases such as "God has reasons we cannot fathom."

When we talk of reasons we are searching for *meaning*, and it is in that realm rather than in the realm of causation that we can more credibly find the hand of God. Later in this section we will try to suggest in some detail how we can perceive the presence of God in the events of our lives. But any expression that indicates that God caused or permitted or could prevent such events is deeply unsatisfactory to many believers.

The traditional belief stems from ancient reflection on the mystery of all that happens in our lives and our communities. People have always felt themselves in the grip of powers stronger than themselves. When we realize that we are not in control of our lives, we try to find out who or what *is* in control, and people have often identified the controlling agent as a god. This discussion is not intended to result in readers' ceasing to believe in God, but rather asks them to reconsider their belief in God as the "puppet master" and to explore in what ways God does indeed influence our lives.

When people ask, "why did my loved one die?" they are often searching for the *causes* of what has happened, and in a way accusing God of causing the death. It is unwise to answer such a question, spoken in crisis, with words; the best answer is shared tears and hugs. At times other than crisis situations, though, a reasonable discussion may be possible. If "why did this person die?" is an inquiry about causality, explanations should be restricted to measurable causes we can identify in the world of phenomena. In the case of disease, the causes may be so minuscule that billions of them can be found in a tiny drop of body fluid. In the case of individual illness or death, doctors or scientists may be able to identify specific causes. "Why did my loved one die?" "Cells ran wild in her body, and medical science couldn't prevent her death." "The person's aorta was 90 percent closed by cholesterol, and the heart could not maintain blood pressure to the body." "The deceased was a passenger when the car was involved in a collision, and the organism was not able to survive the trauma." Such are the perceivable causes of death. They are understandable answers to "why did my loved one die?" They identify causes "in this world." They do not deal with the *meaning* of a person's death, but with the *causes* of death.

When we identify God as the cause of death we are trying to explain what has happened in terms of powers we cannot see, but that we imagine must be involved—and we are doomed to misunderstand. We will more accurately understand God's involvement in our lives if we confine our words about God to language of love and meaning.

There are a great many traditional phrases that imply that God caused a person's death, and all of them are flawed. "God wanted your loved one in heaven." "It is the will of God." "God has a plan for all of us." "God has reasons we can't understand." "Only God decides when a person dies." Perhaps most threatening of all is the platitude, "God will never give you more than you can handle."

No doubt what follows is presumptuous—to express disagreement with each of those familiar statements in a few sentences— but please consider these paragraphs as invitations to reflection, with the added promise that we will soon try again to express in positive language how we *can* find the presence of God in the trials of our lives.

God called your loved one home;
God took your loved one to heaven.

People continue to use traditional phrases indicating that God took a person away from loved ones so that the person could be with God in heaven. To tell a child (of any age) that God took her mother to heaven is to risk an enduring hatred of God. Even some adult children resent God if they believe God's action ended their beloved parent's life at too early a time. If grieving parents of a deceased child ever accepted the suggestion that God took their baby as "one more angel in a court already packed with angels," their rage against God would be overwhelming. Some people may find comfort in words like those, but most people understand such phrases as superstitious and incredible. There may also be an unintended negative effect when they are used, because people who hear them may think: "If this is the best understanding faith has to offer, who can believe?"

Later in this book we will discuss the value of our hope for life beyond death. This series of headings is intended to criticize certain phrases people use to seek meaning about hardship and death: phrases indicating that God caused the hardship, or could prevent the death of a loved one. It is better never to use any phrase that indicates that God caused or permitted or could have prevented the death of someone we love. We just do not understand the real essence of the Spirit of Love if we imagine God as the puppet master who causes everything that happens.

What happened is God's will or God's plan; God has reasons.

When believers look at events and somehow imagine they reveal the existence of a divine plan or "the will of God," we are looking at our own experience and imagining that God must have plans and purposes as humans do. That speculation has been going on since long before biblical times began: people have always accounted for what is hard to explain by attributing events to the planning of an invisible mind. When they won a battle they saw victory as God's will; when they lost, they tried to figure out why God had planned or permitted their defeat.

But surely, when people are struggling to deal with grief, it does not help their faith to imagine that God has willed or planned these events for some unknown reason—to test us? to help us become more mature? to punish us? To think of God's action in this way is traditional, and it may be the best answer people could devise in the face of pain, but to me this understanding is not

credible. It is impossible for me to believe in a God who would
subject creatures to torture to see whether they can cope. God
does not plan hardships for our benefit; God does not have reasons we can never know. We humans imagine that God is somehow like us, making plans and having motives, because our minds
are not capable of understanding the meaning of what has happened to us.

Instead of saying "things happen for a reason," we do better
to say that everything that happens has *meaning*. If "why did this
happen?" represents a search for meaning rather than cause, we
can explore the question to good effect. What made the life of the
deceased person meaningful? Remember the relationships and
activities that enriched the person's life and defined her or his
quest for wholeness. Suffering or death can also be meaningful
for the surrounding network of family and friends: how can we
draw meaning from this event? How were our lives enriched by
knowing this person? What has the person's life and death taught
us about life in general, and our own journeys in particular?

God supports our search for meaning in our lives. God helps
us to deal with the hardships we face with wisdom and courage.
We need to search for God in our pain, but we will find God in
the strength and love (both human and divine) that can result
from the hardship. God is present in our pain as a spiritual force
for good rather than as the cause of our adversity.

Only God decides when a person will die.

This sentence is deeply revered in the Christian community;
it has moral as well as faith-related implications. But it is one
more example of misunderstanding God as the cause of everything that happens in our lives. Rightly understanding that matters of life and death are among the most important that humans
have to face, this sentence tries to reserve issues of life and death
to the sphere of myth. Only an unseen Power has control over
human life and death.

When a middle-aged father and teacher suddenly collapsed and died one evening a few years ago, a pastor tried to console his colleagues and students and the classmates of his children in a school assembly of five hundred people by saying, "It is a mystery. Only God decides when a person dies." The axiom was mutely accepted, but thoughtful reflection must have caused doubt in many hearts. In an atmosphere of grief it does not help a bereaved child or adult to hear that "God decided to deprive you of someone you love." God did not decide that the man would die that evening; God did not cause the death, and God does not prevent heart attacks from achieving their lethal outcome. The *causes* of death should be found in the concrete world, not in an inescapable "puppet master" controlling our destiny. Again, however, we can perceive the presence of God in a sudden death—as the power of love and strength and wisdom helping us to deal with the tragedies that shape our lives.

As the basis of a moral position, the same sentence is used to remove death from the realm of human responsibility. Historically, the church and the state have felt it is within the legitimate power of their leaders to cause the death of human beings "for the good of the wider community." But individual citizens are told they must not make decisions about life and death, because "only God can decide." If, however, God is not the active cause of everyone's death, humans may sometimes have to accept responsibility for decisions about death, as we do for everything else about our lives. Life is one of the greatest human values, deserving of protection by society and by every individual. Still, it is we who are responsible for preserving life, not only God. In some crucial situations we may have to consider whether it may be truly better to choose death rather than life. Obviously, every dilemma must be dealt with in full detail and with due respect for the importance of life. But "leaving it up to God" is an evasion.

God will never give you more than you can bear.

This sentence can be found in the New Testament, in a context of warnings about the consequences of immoral behavior.

> No testing has overtaken you that is not common to
>   everyone.
> God is faithful, and will not let you be tested beyond your
>   strength . . . (1 Corinthians 10:13)

Taken in context, St. Paul's sentence is intended to encourage people to make good decisions lest they find themselves being punished, as God punished their ancestors for evildoing. That type of statement has its own deficiencies as a motivator of good behavior. When the sentence is applied beyond its original context to the issue of bereavement, often it does more harm than good, because sometimes people are indeed "tested beyond their strength" by a tragedy.

Many people, especially when faced with an unexpected and traumatic death, are unable to bear their grief and may suffer psychological breakdown or lasting depression as a result of the death of someone they love. "God will never give you more than you can bear" is a challenge to their faithfulness at a time when they are least able to deal with challenges. It does not help them to be told that God "gave them" this unbearable trial, and that if they would only open their hearts to God's action they could manage their grief. The underlying flaw in the sentence is the image of God handing out disaster to people God deems capable of managing the "test." It is impossible to believe in a God of love who would subject creatures to adversity and claim that if they are true believers they will be able to cope with the trial.

It is valuable for many people to believe that God's strength is available to us in times of crisis. Perhaps the best that can be done, with no underlying implied challenge, is simply to express, with a peaceful and loving spirit, the belief that the tragedy is meaningful both for the person who has died and for those who are left behind. Somehow the God of love is present in the event, not as causing it but as helping us to deal with our grief with wisdom and courage.

We conclude this chapter by reiterating that there are many valuable and credible statements we can make about God's action in our lives (and we have expressed many of them already), but there are many traditional expressions about God that are less credible. Some of those are obvious (God as a warrior inviting people to brutally murder their enemies' children), and some are more acceptable but still deserving of critical reflection. This chapter has been primarily negative, expressing dissatisfaction with some forms of traditional religious teaching. The next chapter will attempt to speak of the actions of God as a spiritual reality, the power of love, in ways that are intended to be more satisfactory for believers.

Reflection Questions

1. What differences in meaning do you perceive between normal processes in nature (for example, the seasons, evaporation and condensation) and natural disasters that affect human lives?

2. Consider the pros and cons of each of the traditional phrases quoted in this chapter that have been used to express the role of God in the tragedies of human life.

Chapter Fifteen

The Power of God Is the Power of Love

If God is not the cause of everything that happens, what is left of our belief? The answer is to be found in the New Testament's profound assertion that God is love.

Grieving believers are sometimes heard to retort, "If God is so loving, why does God allow these terrible things to happen in my life?" Their complaint is based on the lingering concept that God causes or could prevent what happens to us.

What helps me deal with grief is born of the realization that God has long been portrayed as our loving parent. Granted the shortcomings of every comparison, consider the anguish of loving parents who must watch their child succumb to an unconquerable mortal illness. They did not cause the illness; they have tried everything within their power, but they are powerless to prevent it from running its course. Though they love their child completely, they cannot change the course of events. Still, their love for the child and for each other can be healing and transforming, even though it cannot prevent the eventual outcome. Their love may perceive meaning in the horrible brevity of their child's life; their love can give meaning to their own dreadful experience. They may grow in maturity and possibly even in peace of heart through the tragedy. It is not true to say that the experience was imposed on them by God, or to say that if they do not find peace of heart they are rejecting God's help. It *is* true to say that the love of God is very much like the love of those parents: profoundly powerful, healing, meaningful, transforming—but unable to change the circumstances.

The same is true of parents who must watch their adult child make harmful, even life-threatening decisions. Like God, in a way, those loving parents may reach out with advice, with rage, with punishment, with threats, even with forgiveness, but they cannot decide for their child. Even if the young person goes so far as to commit suicide, the heartbroken parents did not cause it; they cannot prevent it, but they still love their child. Can the love of God be any less faithful than the love of human parents, even when people make decisions that are harmful to others and to themselves? God continues to reach out in love, even toward a person who does harm to self and others, but God cannot decide for a person who misuses the gift of freedom.

The presence of the God of love in our lives is very similar to the love of parents facing such dreadful situations. What has *caused* the death-dealing circumstances may be identified by doctors or psychologists, or may be simply unexplainable. What it *means*, how it can affect the human quest for wholeness: that is where the hand of God may be found.

The Power God Has Is the Power of Love

Love is a tremendous power. As discussed in the earlier chapter entitled "God is Love," love gives meaning to life and to events. Love can transform people, heal them, and make them whole; it can help people to grieve with wisdom and courage and to grow through dreadful events they cannot escape.

There are some things that love cannot change. Love does not cause death and love cannot prevent death. Love helps us to be wise and courageous and to try to make sense of even the most difficult aspects of our lives; love unites all the routine activities and the crucial decisions and the times of great joy and the periods of great sorrow. Love propels us on our journey toward wholeness. God is love.

Reflection Questions

This brief chapter attempts to deal with the question, "If God loves us so much, why doesn't God prevent the tragedies that plague our lives?" It is built on the foundation established in chapters entitled "God is Spirit," "God is Love," and "God: The Creator, Not the 'Puppet Master.'"

1. Try to express in your own words the thoughts expressed in this chapter. To what extent do they respond to your understanding of God's role in our lives?

2. Express your acceptance or uncertainty about the statement that God loves us, no matter what happens to us and no matter what we do.

3. Consider the love of parents for a seriously handicapped child. In what ways is their love a profound image of God's love for us?

Chapter Sixteen

Feeling Forsaken by God

"My God, my God, why have you forsaken me?"
(Mark 15:34; Psalm 22:1)

According to the gospels of Matthew and Mark, that agonized cry was the only thing Jesus said while he was dying on the cross. The gospels' portrayal of Jesus' frame of mind as he faced death is disturbing and yet at the same time consoling. Some of us take comfort in realizing that Jesus, the human being who was closest to God of all people who ever lived, apparently felt forsaken and abandoned by God as he faced his death. If we ever find ourselves uncertain of our faith, doubting, feeling abandoned by God, we may take some reassurance in realizing that Jesus himself was affected by feelings of being forsaken by God.

We do know that the words Jesus spoke are the first line of Psalm 22. The psalm is the prayer of a person desperate with fear as he faces death at the hands of enemies. The author prays for deliverance, and eventually, near the end of the long poem, regains a sense of hope and confidence that God is still somehow to be found in the situation. The reading of the entire psalm would doubtless give a more complete picture of the state of Jesus' heart at the moment when he cried out.

Still, the fact remains that the reported words of Jesus on the cross are not the words of a serene and peaceful person. Sometimes feelings of fear and doubt and confusion and distance from God are a natural human reaction to tragedy or bereavement. Such feelings do not indicate that we are bad people, any more than Jesus' reaction indicates that he was not a faithful child of God.

In times of grief many believers try to experience the serenity found in the words of Psalm 23, used so often at funerals. ("The Lord is my shepherd . . . Even though I walk through the darkest valley, I fear no evil; for you are with me.") But when Jesus was facing his own death he did not use the words of Psalm 23. He prayed Psalm 22: "My God, my God, why have you forsaken me?" That psalm is rarely invoked at funerals today.

Serenity is not the only authentic human reaction to grief; distress may be an equally valid human response. Anguish is a natural human emotional reaction to suffering. Often people are unable to feel the comforting presence of God when they suffer tragedy. The process of grieving may take far longer than expected. We may never get over a traumatic loss; the best we can hope for is that we learn to live with it, and through gradual healing are able to regain momentum and begin again to experience positive growth on our journey toward wholeness.

Again, we are all wounded voyagers. Tragedy can mean that we will never become the persons we might have been or might wish to be, but we will become different persons. Some people lose touch with God, as Jesus apparently did; some are unable to restore contact. To feel forsaken by God is not to abandon the journey toward wholeness. It is a measure of how terribly our peace has been disrupted or how deeply we have loved the person we have lost. With or without conscious opening of our heart to God, we may yet redefine ourselves, reaffirm an altered sense of purpose, and resume the long journey toward wholeness.

Reflection Questions

1. How much does it help you to realize that even Jesus himself was not serene when he faced death?

2. Recall situations in which you have (almost) felt abandoned by God. How would you describe the resulting changes in your self-understanding and your sense of what wholeness means for you now?

Chapter Seventeen

The Power of Prayer

> *. . . the Spirit of God helps us in our weakness; for we do not know how to pray as we ought, but the Spirit personally makes our petitions for us in a way that is too deep for words. And God, who can see into all hearts, knows what the Spirit means, because the Spirit pleads with God on behalf of the people and in accordance with God's will.*
>
> (Romans 8:26-27, paraphrased)

Prayer is our human way of getting in touch with the spiritual reality who is God. Often prayer is a reflection on our own lives in awareness of the presence of God, an effort to perceive our lives in an ultimate context—to get the "big picture" about who we are and who God is.

In a small way, all the joys and worries and concerns and hopes of our daily lives are a form of prayer—perhaps even without conscious reference to the presence of God—if we are doing our best to live our whole lives as faithful and prayerful people. When we find ourselves "distracted" by the problems of our lives while we are trying to pray or are participating in common worship, perhaps even the distractions are a type of prayer as we struggle with the realities of our lives in the presence of God.

Sometimes we consciously and seriously reflect on our lives in awareness of God's presence, pondering what wholeness truly means for us, and what progress we are making in the long journey of life. In that setting we may well find ourselves overwhelmed by the greatness of the God of love. God gives meaning to our amazing world and our very complex lives. God supports us in our lifelong quest for wholeness. God empowers us to live as God's faithful people, to grow in love, to be wise, to make good decisions, and to have the courage to do what we know is right. God promises to forgive us when we recognize that we have failed—and in that very forgiveness God heals us and leads us ever onward toward wholeness.

The mystery that is God is far more complex than anything we can know in our world, but we hope to experience the reality of God more and more deeply through our prayer and reflection. We want to find true ways of affirming God's greatness, but at the same time we sometimes feel dissatisfied with some expressions about God. Even so, the search is prayerful, and our deepest reaction may be anything from confusion to hope, thanksgiving, and praise.

As Paul writes in the quotation at the beginning of this chapter, we do not know how to pray as we should, but we believe that the Spirit of God lives within us and knows us better than we know ourselves. Somehow our reflections and worries and fears and hopes are literally communication "in a way that is too deep for words" with the God who lives within us.

Prayer of Petition

One type of prayer we have been taught, but that causes uncertainty for many people, is the prayer that asks God to intervene in our lives and change our circumstances. It is undeniably valuable for us to articulate our needs, to recognize our weakness and helplessness, to express our hopes, and to feel the presence of God in our yearnings. But we should not see our prayer as an effort to "change God's mind" and to solicit some kind of magical intervention to relieve us of a circumstance that is afflicting us. Rather, the best prayer asks that God may change *us*—heal us, transform us, make us wise and courageous, lead us on toward wholeness. Rather than praying that God give food to people who are starving, for example, we ought to pray that God will inspire us to take action, however small, to relieve people's suffering.

Some parts of the preceding paragraphs will be very troubling for many, and indeed will be rejected by many readers, but thoughtful believers have struggled with the issue for centuries. We need to explore the value of petition prayer and express it in a way that is credible for us. The thoughts in the preceding paragraphs have been expressed in various ways by reflective believers as long ago as St. Thomas Aquinas, a great Roman Catholic theologian who lived in the thirteenth century.

To present the traditional understanding in an admittedly simplistic way, we were taught as children to imagine God up in heaven receiving millions of prayerful requests and deciding which ones are worthy of miraculous intervention. Even when we were praying for something that seemed eminently worthwhile to us, we were told that God might understand things differently. People through the ages have been assured that God hears and answers every prayer, though not always in a way we can perceive or understand; some of those people have been able to live with disappointment that things did not turn out the way they hoped.

That idea is very hard for believers to accept when they are asking God to change the behavior of an abuser, or to save an indispensable loved one from death, or to relieve a disastrous famine or drought. Rationalizations may be proposed about why God "refuses" to save the life of a mother of young children or does not send rain to prevent the starvation of millions of African people, but for many the rationalizations are not convincing. It is very hard to believe in a God who loves people and could relieve their anguish, and yet chooses not to.

Years ago, a young Canadian, Terry Fox, lost a leg to cancer. He recovered enough to attempt literally to run across Canada with one prosthetic leg. His valiant Marathon of Hope came to an end after more than three thousand miles when the cancer returned. Students in those days wanted to pray for him to recover from the cancer that had now been diagnosed as terminal. But many adults knew that Terry was sure to die, and we felt that his death might have had a harmful effect on the faith of young people if they imagined that God was up in heaven listening to the prayers of millions of Canadian children and adults and rejecting those pleas. We felt it was much better to pray, united in love, that Terry would realize how much he was loved and would find peace in his suffering, and that his family would find God in the bonds of love and wisdom that united them with Terry. Twenty years of strong social initiatives have shown that his family did indeed draw strength and meaning from Terry's death; they have done immeasurable good around the world in uniting people in the battle against cancer.

There are many groups of believers in our world who are entirely convinced of the power of prayer in the belief that it brings about miraculous interventions of God in selected cases. Without denying that remarkable outcomes do at times occur, I prefer to use the word "unexplainable," rather than to believe that those outcomes are the result of the direct intervention of a "puppet master" God. Regrettably, some prayer groups are oppressive in their conviction about the power of prayer. If a member asks prayers for the recovery of a terminally ill person, the leader may inquire, "Are you asking for a cure?" If the member responds positively, the attitude of the leader may be expressed as, "If you really believe, and pray with all your heart, your loved one will be cured." When the sick person dies, the member is led to believe that the death is the result of inadequate faith or prayer. In my view, such an attitude is tyrannical.

The whole idea that petition prayer can result in measurable symptomatic change is based on a flawed human understanding about God as causing everything that happens in our lives and as being able to prevent all the hardship that happens in the world. We have explored that understanding in the previous chapter. We must find a more credible way of expressing the action of God in our lives. The more credible understanding is based on the biblical saying that God is love.

The Power of Prayer Is the Power of Love

It is good for us to recognize our needs and our helplessness, and to express our hopes both inwardly and aloud. It is good for us to pray for each other, expressing what we hope, and united in the bond of love that is the presence of God. When we pray, united in the spirit of love, our prayer has power. We really do help each other, and God really does strengthen us. Love has marvelous transforming and healing effects. Sometimes people experience good results of others' prayers even when they do not know they are being prayed for.

But it is not accurate to imagine God as a sort of gift-giving Santa Claus, magically manipulating phenomena "down here on earth." Rather, we should imagine God as the power of love and wisdom and courage and meaning, who dwells within us and around us. We have already discussed the limitations of what love can do—as, for example, with the love of parents watching their baby's life ebb away as the result of a mortal illness.

What love *does* do is help us to find meaning to our journey, transform our inner lives, lead us on toward wholeness—no matter what circumstances we are in, no matter whether we live or die, no matter what happens to us. The God of love is with us and within us, and that is what ultimately helps us to live meaningful lives, enables us to be wise and courageous, and leads us toward wholeness. That is the essence of what prayer can do. The power of prayer is the power of love.

Reflection Questions

1. Express what prayer will mean for you if you accept the idea that God is not manipulating events that happen in the world, but is a real and transforming factor in our lives in the areas of wisdom and love.

Chapter Eighteen

God Who Conquers Death

Our quest for wholeness will come to its conclusion when we die. At that moment we will recognize and celebrate the truth about ourselves—the person we have built with the help of God and other people, by means of a lifetime of loving and being loved, of reaffirming our purpose, of making responsible decisions, of growing in freedom, and of developing in emotional well-being. At death we will face the reality of our shortcomings and give thanks for the life we have lived and the person we have become.

Further, we believe that we will continue to be sustained by the saving love of God, even beyond our death. Jesus spoke about life beyond death in terms of resurrection. "I will raise you up on the last day" is a phrase that is found only in John's gospel, but it expresses what one early Christian community understood about Jesus' teaching with regard to life beyond death. The letters of Paul and the first three gospels also refer to the hope for resurrection, using images that speak of both continuity and transformation: like the risen Jesus, we will continue to be the persons we are, but we will be entirely changed.

The resurrection Jesus spoke about is not based on the dualistic Greek idea of an immortal soul living on in a heaven of souls and is not a "coming back to life as it was before death." Rather, resurrection refers to a transformation of the person to a remarkably different way of living.

The Resurrection of Jesus

The narratives that tell of the resurrection of Jesus portray both continuity and transformation in assuring us that Jesus lives beyond his death. Some of the narratives make it clear that "it is the same Jesus we knew." In one scene Jesus cooks breakfast for his followers over a campfire and eats with them (John 21:9-14); in another, he invites Thomas to put his fingers into the nail holes (John 20:27; see Luke 24:39). Those episodes indicate continuity: the disciples experienced the presence of their friend Jesus after his death. In other accounts, however, Jesus' best friends look right at him (John 20:14-16), or walk with him for hours (Luke 24:13-35), without recognizing him. Those stories emphasize transformation: Jesus is different than he was before.

The narrative about the disciples on the road to Emmaus (Luke 24:13-35) responds to questions that are asked by searching believers today as they were asked by third-generation Christians in the first century: "How can I know that Jesus has risen to new life? Why should I believe? Where can I find him?" The narrative tells about two friends of Jesus, walking away from Jerusalem after Jesus has been killed. A stranger joins them and explains the Scriptures referring to a suffering Messiah. When they have supper together, the stranger breaks bread and gives thanks for it, and then vanishes when they recognize him. It is a narrative about transformation: the story implies that Jesus after resurrection is very different than he was before his death. The Gospel of Luke offers a brilliant threefold response to the question, "Where can I find him?" "Open your eyes! He is walking right beside you and you don't even recognize him!" "He can be found in the word of God, properly understood." And "he is present in the breaking of the bread, the Eucharist." Jesus is indeed alive in our world, but not in the same form as before his death. He lives a transformed spiritual life now and is present to us as God is present in our world. "Blessed are those who have not seen and yet have come to believe" (John 20:29).

Our Hope for Resurrection

The earliest Christian document we possess, Paul's first letter to the Christians at Thessalonica (1 Thessalonians 4:14), proclaims that when they die, believers will follow the path taken by Jesus after his death: "For since we believe that Jesus died and rose again, even so, through Jesus, God will bring with him those who have died." The first letter to the Corinthians (1 Corinthians 15:35-37, 42-44) offers a comparison to express the continuity and transformation that characterize life after death. Paul reflects on the transformation of a seed as it grows into a plant: the plant is completely different from the seed; the seed has been transformed. Who could look at a sunflower seed for the first time and imagine that somehow within that seed is a tall green plant topped by a large golden flower? Yet it is the same life: the mature plant is somehow in the seed. The form it will take when fully grown cannot be imagined simply by looking at the seed. Paul compares our life on earth to the seed. What our transformed life will be like beyond death is unimaginable. Still, we cannot resist trying to imagine it, trying to say something true about this mystery.

In spite of our uncertainty about details, Christian tradition affirms that we will maintain our identity after death, that God will be fully present to us, and that we will be fully present to God and to one another in the networks of love that began during our mortal life. We will be the same persons, but we will be dramatically changed; we will live in a totally new way after resurrection. Like Jesus, we will live with God; we will live as God lives. God is a spiritual being. God is real and powerful, everywhere and forever. We are and will continue to be images of God.

We who live in the world of time must wait to be reunited with our loved ones who have died. The dead, however, are beyond time and place.

Beyond death and resurrection we will be free of time, as God is. "Free of time" means free of limitations. We will not have to worry about being "on time," as we must so often on earth; we will not have to wait, patiently or impatiently, for joyful life to continue. We will not be bored doing nothing for a long time. We will live in a different way after death and resurrection, perhaps describable as a continuing "now," always "happening." When we pray in the world of time for our departed loved ones, they are helped "beyond time" by our prayers. Perhaps they are helped even before their death or at the time of their death. Perhaps, since beyond death there is no time, we should imagine that the resurrection of the dead happens at the "moment of truth," when we face the reality of the person we have created with God's help. That person will live forever.

Heaven is not best understood as a *place* we go to after death. "Where are our deceased loved ones?" That question can best be answered by repeating the questions discussed earlier: "Where is God?" "Where is love?" Since God/love is within us and all around us, it seems eminently faithful to perceive the continued presence of our dear departed in our lives.

Life after death is a different way of being, defined simply as living in complete union with God. Pope John Paul II spoke of heaven as a new dimension of being, defined in Paul's words as being "with the Lord forever" (1 Thessalonians 4:17). We will continue to be ourselves, and yet our lives will be changed for the better. We will live with God; we will live as God lives. We will renew our relationships with people we have known and loved on earth, without fear of jealousy or separation or loss. We will be happy; we will not be alone. Such is our hope, because we trust in the love of Jesus.

Nothing Can Separate Us from the Love of God

Perhaps a personal statement is appropriate to conclude the discussion of this most delicate of topics.

Hope for life beyond death is something that cannot be "proven." Some thoughtful searchers believe that the hope for an afterlife may have developed across a wide variety of civilizations because of people's enduring wish that the unfairness and misery of human life will be redressed in a life beyond the grave. It feels strange to say that if true wholeness does consist in what was described in the first half of this book, I could be content with having lived an authentic life, whether that life continues beyond death or not. Loving and being loved, living with a sense of purpose, trying to live according to true values, feeling inwardly free no matter the circumstances, and growing in emotional well-being—all these factors will combine into a sense of—admittedly imperfect—fulfillment and wholeness at the time of my death.

Still, especially because of the death of my beloved wife (and also because of my subsequent marriage), and because of my deep bond with my children and my interest in their lives and loves, I want to believe in life after death. I believe that death is not the end of human life.

I hope that we will be transformed and live in some unimaginable way with God. I believe that we will retain our identity and continue our networks of love in a way that is only joyful and has none of the tensions that afflict human relationships in the world of time. I can imagine all sorts of adventures that might be possible for spirit-beings, but I realize they are only conjecture.

I find comfort in the words of St. Paul that follow. I believe, as Paul writes, that nothing can separate us from the active, unconditional love of God, who reaches into our lives, gives them meaning, and leads us to wholeness. No matter what happens to us, and no matter what we do, nothing in the world, not even death, can ever separate us from the love of God.

We know that all things work together for good for those who love God . . . I am convinced that neither hardships nor distress, neither death nor life, nothing already in existence and nothing still to come, nor any power, nor anything else in all creation, *nothing* will be able to separate us from the love of God, which is made known to us in Christ Jesus our Lord. (Romans 8:28, 38-39, partly paraphrased)

Reflection Questions

1. What questions do you have about the resurrection of Jesus? To what extent do the brief ideas in this chapter help to respond to these questions? If you wish to read more on the topic, do not rely only on the Internet for information, but search for books from your own faith tradition.

2. To what extent can you find hope in simple statements and unanswered questions about life beyond death such as those presented in this chapter?

Epilogue

"The time is fulfilled, and the kingdom of God has come near."
(Mark 1:15)

"Today salvation has come to this house."
(Luke 19:9)

"Your faith has made you whole."
(Mark 5:34)

The coming of the reign of God was Jesus' most important teaching. His proclamation means that if we allow God to reign in our hearts, God will transform our lives. That action of God is expressed by the term salvation. "God saves us" means that God reaches into our lives and leads us toward wholeness. That is the Good News proclaimed in the New Testament.

In this book we have discussed some of the factors that contribute to our wholeness: awareness of being loved, a sense of ultimate purpose, a consistent personal value system, freedom and emotional well-being. Whatever our circumstances, the extent to which these factors have been realized in our lives is the extent to which we will consider our lives to have been authentic and fulfilling.

In the second half of the book we have proposed language about God that is worthy of belief, after having identified some ways of speaking of God that may be considered inadequate. God knows us and loves us for who we are and sets us free to be true to ourselves. God helps us to be wise and to make sense of our lives; God supports us as we try to make good choices and to have the courage to do what we know is right; God forgives us when we sin and offers to overcome our failures, heal us, and lead us ever onward toward wholeness. God's saving love does not end at our death. If we are open to the transforming power of God we will succeed in our lifelong quest for wholeness.

Acknowledgments

The initial inspiration for the first half of this book was a comment by Gordon Taylor, a now-retired teacher and school principal. Gord noticed that the word "wholeness" appeared frequently in my introductory book about the Bible, *Language of the Heart*,[1] and he asked simply, "What is wholeness?" This book is an attempted response, and I thank Gord for the question.

I have learned about faith and life from many discussions with searching people in a variety of settings. Continuing insight has come from teachers taking courses in Religious Education at the York Catholic District School Board north of Toronto, and from my colleagues, the other instructors of those courses, under the leadership of Patrick Collins and Denise Dupuis.

In recent years I have been involved with a remarkable ecumenical Scripture study group in Toronto. For a quarter of a century more than sixty people have been attending lectures about the Scriptures in series of ten talks every autumn and ten more talks every winter. All of the participants are almost as old as or older than I am. They are remarkably open-minded and thoughtful, and their attitude gainsays any stereotypes of our generation as inflexible. Their questions and insight have broadened my horizons significantly.

---

[1] Noel Cooper, *Language of the Heart: How to Read the Bible* (Ottawa: Novalis, 2003).

Another source of wisdom, especially about the challenges of parenting, has come from the participants in Focus on Fathers, a program developed by Ed Bader, who has been an innovative and resourceful marriage and family counselor for many decades.

Drafts of this book were improved by the comments of The Rev. William A. Gilbert, an Anglican priest in Ottawa; Kathleen Lavin, a voracious reader and member of the ecumenical study group; and my wife Pat Beecham-Cooper, an award-winning teacher.

I have very much appreciated the services of Hans Christofferson, the Editorial Director of Liturgical Press, and his staff.

Finally, guidance and inspiration for my own personal quest for wholeness have come from my family: my wife Pat; my three sons, Andrew, Paul, and John (to whom this book is dedicated); and their loving wives, Lauren, Sarah, and Kate.

To all these contributors to my education and my journey, thank you sincerely.

I would be happy to hear comments and discuss issues related to this book. Readers are welcome to get in touch at nhpcoop@yahoo.ca.

Noel Cooper
December 21, 2008
The winter solstice
The first day of Hanukkah
The fourth Sunday of Advent